Don't Smile
until Christmas

Accounts of
the First Year of Teaching
Edited by
Kevin Ryan

Don't Smile
until
Christmas

With contributions by
John Canfield
Linda Corman
Gary Cornog
Wylie Crawford
Eleanor Fuke
Gail Richardson
Kevin Ryan

The University of Chicago Press
Chicago and London

The title of the first chapter, "To Care and Not to Care," and the two lines of poetry which follow it are reproduced from T. S. Eliot's "Ash Wednesday" by permission of Harcourt, Brace and World, Inc. The chapter entitled "Hangman or Victim" contains part of a speech from *The Persecution and Assassination of Jean-Paul Marat as Performed by the Inmates of the Asylum of Charenton under the Direction of the Marquis de Sade,* a play by Peter Weiss, © 1965 by John Calder Ltd., reproduced with the permission of the author, Atheneum Publishers, and Calder and Boyars Ltd.

The names of the persons and schools referred to in these papers have been changed.

International Standard Book Number: 0–226–73230–4
Library of Congress Catalog Card Number: 72–103428

The University of Chicago Press, Chicago 60637
The University of Chicago Press, Ltd., London

This book is dedicated to
            those who would join the ranks of

    the chalk-soiled,
                    ink-stained,

        over-
        challenged,

                un   supported,
                der-

                        memo-ridden,
        privacy-riddled,

        patience-worn, school-fatigued,

                lovers of children and ideas.

Contents

Introduction   ix
Kevin Ryan

To Care and Not to Care   1
Gary Cornog

White Teacher, Black School   25
John Canfield

X Is for the Unknown   60
Gail Richardson

The Other Side of the Coin   80
Wylie Crawford

Hangman or Victim   103
Linda Corman

Identity or Discipline   128
Eleanor Fuke

The First Year of Teaching   164
Kevin Ryan

Introduction

Most would agree that a liberal education alone does not make a teacher. Nor do education courses. Nor does student teaching. These are all preparations for the actual experience that forms a teacher—the first year of teaching. The process of becoming a teacher is complicated because the new teacher is not simply entering a profession. He is also starting another phase of his life. He is entering the adult world. He has to negotiate a new role within the larger society. He becomes a taxpayer and a voter. Normally, he leaves home and must establish himself in a strange community. He must find a place to live, to bank, to buy groceries. He begins to think about things like buying a car and life insurance. He must make new friends. If he has not just married, he begins the search in earnest. So many of the daily concerns that were taken care of by parents and his college community, he must now take on alone. For some, the process is exhilarating; for others, painful. For all, it is new and demanding.

Each year tens of thousands of college graduates leave the campus to enter secondary schools as first-year teachers. They enter with high hopes and vague uncertainties. Schools as institutions are no surprise to them. They have been through them and know much about life in classrooms. They are aware of the rules, the customs, and the taboos of the schools, though only—it is true —from having been on the receiving end. And while they may not be scholars, their knowledge of their subject fields extends well beyond that of their students. Still, the transition from student to teacher is a jolting experience.

This book had its origins in that problem of transition. All too often the first-year teachers asked me, "Why didn't you tell us what it was like out there?" I had tried, but it is difficult to present prospective teachers with an authentic picture of the experience of becoming a teacher. When teacher educators try, they fail frequently and for a variety of reasons. Sometimes their graphic pictures of the first year of teaching are too inconsistent with the prospective teacher's fantasy of success. Sometimes the teacher educators' view of the schools is out-of-date. The professional literature is not very helpful here either; the true life of the school slips through the nets of research studies. Except for rare instances, novelists have failed to capture the essence of school; the teacher and his student are highly romanticized in fiction and provide little real guidance for the beginning teacher. Still, I kept hearing, "Why didn't you tell us what it's really like out there?" And then I heard a beginner say, "I could write a book about what's happened in my seventh period this year." I realized I had the beginnings of an answer.

The title of this book may be puzzling to some, but in the teaching profession it is a shopworn piece of folklore. It is quite common for a beginning teacher to be taken aside by a senior colleague and given the advice, "Don't smile until Christmas." The meaning is, "Be very careful to keep a tight rein on yourself if you hope to keep control of your classes." Implicit in the advice is the assumption that if you smile, and in effect appear friendly, your class may take advantage of you and not allow you to teach. If, on the other hand, rigid discipline is enforced during the first few months, a set of rules and a tone will be set for the class, and the students will be "whipped into shape." Then you can afford to ease up. The prevalence of this piece of advice is in itself a telling commentary on the American secondary school. That so many teachers are not guided by educational theory or research-based knowledge, but swear by such folklore, attests to the credibility gap within the teaching profession.

This book is intended especially for those who are contemplating becoming teachers. Its aim is simply to allow the prospective high school teacher to get inside the skin of six beginning teachers, to feel what they have felt, to experience what they have experienced. In mind, too, are those in their first year of teaching. It is hoped that they will receive some solace when they discover that they are not alone. Experienced teachers may find these accounts of the first year of teaching nostalgic; they may bring back the memories of those early triumphs and defeats. The lay public, those to whom the schools belong, will find in this book a rare view of what it is like to serve in the schools. For all of us, however, the book should raise some questions about the teaching profession and particularly the profession's induction system.

The composite landscape of the first year of teaching that this book presents is not altogether pleasant. The authors' accounts are honest, personal, and hypersensitive. Some will find the authors' hopes and expectations for the schools themselves unrealistic. Nevertheless, this is how six beginners perceive their first year. They insist, "This is how it is." Some will wonder why more is not made of their satisfactions. Perhaps they had few satisfactions. Possibly a more psychologically accurate answer is that frustrations and disappointments of the kind they experienced were new to them. Being new experiences, they dominated their writing.

To fully understand the behavior of these six beginning teachers and their reaction to the schools, we must realize that they are part of a generation with high expectations for life. They are part of a generation which has had a comfortable, affluent youth, particularly by the standards of the past. They are part of a generation whose social conscience has been sharpened by an ugly, confusing war, by political assassinations, by racial injustices, and by a vivid awareness of poverty. They are part of a generation with a deep sense of human potential, human suffering, and human injustice. They are impatient. They put little stock in the way things have been or are. They have little faith in institutions. All of this came to a head when they became teachers. Their work in the school has been their greatest personal challenge and, for some, their first nose-to-nose confrontation with our society's ills.

The six beginning teachers were selected for this project because they were representative of different personality types, teaching fields, and school settings. Only six were invited to participate, and all persevered to completion. Three are young women and three are young men. The five schools in which they taught serve communities on a spectrum from wealthy all-white suburbs to predominantly black inner-city schools. All six were in the second, or internship phase of an experimental, two-year master of arts in

teaching program at the University of Chicago. Although most
of them had a somewhat reduced teaching load and were supervised by university faculty members, they all looked upon their
internship as their first year of teaching. And indeed, it was. One
wonders what would have been their reaction if they had had the
added pressure of a full teaching load and no university supervision.

They graduated with liberal arts degrees from some of the
nation's finest schools: Antioch, Columbia, Cornell, Harvard, the
University of Portland, and Vassar. One spent a year with VISTA,
and another with a civil rights group in the South. All spent an
additional year at the University of Chicago prior to their internship. During this year at the university they took specially designed education courses, and advanced graduate courses in their
teaching field, and they had some teaching experiences in the University Laboratory Schools. These highly qualified and carefully
selected teachers had the kind of academic training and teacher
preparation which few beginning teachers are fortunate enough
to have. They are representative of the very best talent entering
teaching today. Still, as the first six chapters make clear, their
entrance was not smooth and was not without trauma.

In the concluding chapter, I try to pull together some of the
central themes of the preceding six accounts. While it is difficult,
if not dangerous, to generalize from the experiences of six beginners, I am convinced their experiences are not radically different
from those of most beginners. Since there is such a paucity of
research on the first year of teaching, I was forced to draw heavily
on my own six years of work with beginning teachers. There
should be no doubt about it, though: the chapter is biased. It is
written from deep conviction that we do a very crude job of preparing and inducting people into the teaching profession. I suspect
our progeny will look from the 21st century at our training programs for teachers and cluck their tongues in dismay. They will
probably view our current practices the way we look upon the
training of doctors during that period when they used leeches and
blood letting. Whether or not this be true is unimportant. We
only have control over now. If we are to have fine schools manned
by superior teachers, changes must be made. It is hoped that the
candid revelations of these six beginners will cause us to question
and, finally, to act.

Many people helped in the writing of this book. Besides the authors being a great stimulus to one another, numerous outsiders gave help and support. William Lauroesch, Alice Carnes, Earl Seidman, Donald Edgar, and Roger Pillet, all gave valuable advice on the final chapter. Roald Campbell, the dean of the Graduate School of Education, was a continuing source of encouragement. Three people, in particular, were of great assistance in typing the various drafts in the final copy. They are Evada Waller, Lydia Elliott, and Vicky Leak.

It is standard for an author to make generous references to his wife's contribution to a book. I can honestly say, however, that this book would not be in print without the assistance of my wife, Marilyn. She did much more than the usual wifely duties of making coffee and keeping the baby quiet. She was in on the conception of the book. She worked with the contributors, helping them to sharpen their manuscripts, and in some cases their perceptions. She pointed out areas we were overlooking or overdoing. When I got discouraged or bored with the project, she reminded me that it was important. And she made coffee and kept the baby quiet.

KEVIN RYAN

Gary Cornog

To Care
and Not to Care

Teach us to care and not to care
Teach us to sit still.
          T. S. Eliot, "Ash Wednesday"

A year or so before I began facing a classroom on a daily basis, I had the idea that teaching English would be a series of extended Socratic dialogues between me and my students. I would educate in the thoroughly etymological sense: I would *lead forth* my eager, responsive, naïve but (redeemingly) idealistic students from the cave of adolescent mental wistfulness into the clear light of Truth upon the verdant and lush fields of literature.

My experience of two weeks of practice teaching in the Laboratory School of the University of Chicago should in some way have indicated the serious discrepancy between my expectations of teaching and the somewhat less rosy reality of the situation, but I rationalized that uncomfortable deduction out of all consideration by telling myself that my Lab School students were mere eighth graders, that they in no way could represent the level of maturity and sophistication I would be encountering in the suburban setting of my high school. My rationalization was not entirely without truth. In going from high primary to secondary education I found the difference in maturity to be that which exists between proto- and pure pubescence, and the difference in sophistication to be indicated by the respective popularity of "Peanuts" and *Candy*.

School began for me in a well-to-do Chicago suburb the day after Labor Day 1967. That holiday's name seems particularly symbolic now that I reflect on it from the distance of a completed year of teaching. In my teacher-infancy, trailing clouds of glory from the University of Chicago (my intellectual foster home—

1

or incubator, to be more appropriately egg-headish), scarcely
weaned from classroom complacency learned through years of
student status, I was now what I had before been able to regard
with distant indifference, mild admiration, or hearty dislike—a
teacher. In much the same way that each of us thinks of disaster
and death as being some calamity which affects others but never
ourselves, so I thought of the term "teacher." Despite the fact
that my father and brother had preceded me in this field (I almost
said "death"), I was unable and unwilling to envision myself as
"one of them." To me the word "teacher" connoted "nonentity."
Somehow this distaste I had for the term did not taint the gratifications I expected to receive from acting in the capacity of a
teacher of English. In the classroom, or so it then seemed to
me, individual styles and procedures would effectively obliterate
stereotyping. My students and I would both see that I was not like
all other teachers. How true! How false! But I'm anticipating—

My first class on that first day met in mid-morning; hence, I
had nearly three hours in which to assist the creation of ulcers
and lung cancer through the gastric distress brought on by hyper-
tension and the fictitious calming influence of cigarettes. The
time came (as I knew it had to, even though I cherished a faint
hope that perhaps a fire or even an errant inland hurricane might
cause the closing of the school for several weeks); and I, a smile
denoting grim friendliness affixed to my face, bearing myself as
casually as any novice, went forth to meet my students.

After I had taken ten minutes to take the roll (a stalling tactic),
I thought I might engage the class in the first of our no doubt
numberless discussions on topics of general interest. Because of
the forces of psychic repression which routinely whirl into action
in traumatic situations, I can no longer recall the exact subject I
brought up for discussion. All that I remember is the ominous, dull
Nothing which filled the room after I had asked one or two general questions. Several months later, while watching a BBC production of E. M. Forster's *A Passage to India,* I found the perfect
analogy to my impression in the response of Mrs. Moore and Miss
Quested to their confrontation with the Marabar caves. No matter
what one said inside those caves, no matter what language was
used, the response was always the same—a dull, hollow moan.
So also in my classes those first (and many subsequent) days. The
"cave" out of which I was to lead my students seemed to confound

my intentions by distorting or devouring my directions. *Mutatis mutandis* I went from the Socrates Plato depicts in the *Republic* to the farcical one Aristophanes mocked in *The Clouds*. This wasn't at all the way things were supposed to be, I told myself; and then, in soothing sessions of self-pity, I indulged myself in the convenient pastime of blaming my students for causing my disappointment. I reflected on the immense gap of ignorance which separated them from me.

It was not just an ignorance of subject matter; that was to be expected. It was rather the ignorance these students had of me which contributed to my self-pity. What I had hoped would not occur had happened before I began to teach: my students responded to me as to a cardboard figure who wore the label "English teacher." Despite their gradually increasing familiarity with me as an individual, they would still react as Lenin would have liked the proletariat to have acted in Europe—*en masse*. In short, my students—at all times objectively, and occasionally also subjectively—possessed a class consciousness, an awareness of who they were, which enabled or, more correctly, forced them to define me as an "other." This discrimination which they made was not personally directed against me, although I initially thought it was. Instead, it was a conditioned response which years of authoritarian schooling had ingrained in their minds. I too, without thinking, had acted in the same general way when I was their age. It was not until that way of behaving was directed toward me that I began to realize what is really upsetting about teaching—the indifference of one's students.

I felt grieved at the apparent misunderstanding being made by my students. They too hastily put me in a category. I was not a typical teacher. I was going to be enlightened and relevant, lenient and considerate. An atmosphere of mutual respect would characterize our classroom. English for my students would be a welcome respite from the dull ordinariness of their other courses. In reaction to their typing of me, however, I found myself feebly attempting to compromise my image of myself with their picture of a teacher. Blurred and ill-defined, the vague shape of a disciplinarian superimposed itself menacingly on my mental image of myself. My students had trumped my Dr. Jekyll with Mr. Hyde. I saw that the time was coming when I would have to cash in my Mr. Chips.

To a great extent, then, I found my first year of teaching to be a period during which I gradually became accustomed to the problem of pedagogical schizophrenia—the phenomenon of reconciling two personalities: the human being and the disciplinarian *in loco parentis.* As a consequence of this, the recurrent topic of this narrative will be tensions I found to be present in my classes. These tensions were of several varieties; basically they were caused by the discrepancy between what the class was doing and the way I wanted the class to act. Occasionally I would find myself in a situation similar to that in *The Sorcerer's Apprentice,* with myself in the title role. Somehow I would have pushed the wrong button or said the wrong thing, and suddenly the whole class would be out of control. Perhaps I had shown some recognition of a lewd reference. Perhaps I had allowed myself to indulge in some mild bantering. Maybe I had forced a double meaning into a student's reply to one of my questions. Whatever the catalyst might have been, the reaction, from the standpoint of a "work-oriented" classroom environment, was usually regrettable.

More frequent than these lapses into chaos caused by some overt gesture on my part were the lapses brought about by my failure to plan my daily lessons sufficiently well to fill up the allotted time. Often I would run out of questions to ask the class; and while I stood in front of them, awkwardly groping for another question, I would notice a pair of students in one corner of the room beginning a conversation, another student reaching for his algebra book, another becoming interested in the activities going on in the courtyard below our class. If the question for which I was searching had not been found by this time, I would soon have to resort to a frantic blustering of commands for silence and attention. Naturally the students felt something was wrong when, after reestablishing order, I did not continue with my series of questions. Gradually, over the course of the year, I learned to ask questions according to a descending order of generality. In the beginning I had failed to think of sufficiently general questions. Instead of discussing the thematic content of *Macbeth,* I would ask my students to paraphrase a certain speech or make sense out of a certain line. Since we spent nine weeks on this play, only rarely receiving relief in the form of films, it was not surprising that a staleness should have begun to affect our attitudes toward English by the midpoint of the first semester.

My one senior class was to begin the year of American literature with some selected works of Jonathan Edwards and Ben-
jamin Franklin. Fool that I was, I thought Edwards' sermons
could be discussed on the same level that Edwards wrote them—
that of abstract concepts concerning matters of salvation and
damnation. Even if a student did not fully comprehend Edwards'
particular scriptural interpretation, at least his Sunday school
indoctrination would have acquainted him with some basic tenets
of Christianity. At least the student would be able to recognize
the relatedness of Edwards to religion, thought I. For the most
part I was mistaken in this assumption. The seniors, affected with
a far more serious case of assumed coolness than the juniors,
could not seem to believe that they were being called upon to
discuss religious issues in their English class. To them, Edwards
was a nut. Franklin? He was different. Franklin was practical;
he realized you had to compromise and conform in order to survive in the world. He was far more American than Edwards, said
the seniors. And so began another source of tension. Throughout
the year, the seniors and I kept encountering new veins of the
same deposit in American literature—the split in the American
character between other-worldly idealism and mysticism (the
writings of Edwards, Hawthorne, Melville, Dickinson, Whitman,
Thoreau, and Emerson, to name a few), and the very worldly,
practical, realistic, business-success-oriented outlook found in
Franklin and parodied elsewhere in our literature. I willingly
became an advocate and defendant for the former category; my
students readily presented the case for the latter.

When my attempt to discuss Edwards theologically met with
failure, I tried a new approach. Why not try to see if I can induce
in my students an awareness that many of the values they held
dear in their hearts were but tubers on the great subterranean
root of Puritan thought? With this in mind, I spent a day discussing the idea of Success. What did the word mean to them? Was
success something that could be measured? Was it a material
concept or a spiritual one? They were entirely comfortable with
these abstractions. I became more specific.

"Would you consider yourself successful if you earned a salary
of $10,000?"

"It would depend on the job I had," said one boy.

"What if you were a social worker?"

"No."

"A teacher?"

"Maybe."

"A truck driver?"

"No."

"A junior executive freshly graduated from a business school?"

"Yes."

"So," said I, "your idea of success is based principally on your idea of status, right?" (I was really sounding like Socrates now, I thought.)

"Right," said the boy.

Of course it was an easy series of questions from this point to the clincher: "You therefore conceive of success as something which can be measured materially, correct?"

"Correct."

By this time the majority of the class had lost interest in the dialectical process. For me, however, it had been a small triumph —like bidding and making five spades or some cognate thrill of this petty ilk. The pettiness of it appeared clearer to me when I reflected upon it later. Then I saw that I was acting in a somewhat self-aggrandizing manner. "Look how much more clever I am than you are!" seemed to be the tone I was taking in my questioning. Like some ruthless D.A. on television, I was carving up a witness for the benefit of the jury and the audience.

My first few weeks of futility with *Macbeth* in the junior classes and with Puritan thought in the senior class were not relieved when I contemplated the prospect which lay ahead of me. After Edwards, American literature seemed like a vast, hideous wasteland sparsely covered with stunted trees and unrelieved desolation—an intellectual Nevada—before an author of interest would provide us with an oasis. (Hawthorne, alas, seemed more like a mirage.) I would first have to slog through my colonial literati, then Irving and Poe, then Bryant (I decided to skip him), then Emerson (poor Waldo—so profound, so up-tight on Nature, so un-cool—I would have a hard time justifying the ways of Emerson to my seniors), then Thoreau ("He must be a communist!" they'll say, I know it; at any rate he's subversive), and finally to Melville. Oh, and of course the *Scarlet Letter;* I almost forgot that one. The menu of our literature would not be complete without that entrée: one has not had a high school education in

America unless one has had a pinch of Prynne and a dollop of Dimmesdale.

More characteristic of my senior class than the calculating cross-examination were those days during which my self-esteem suffered severe setbacks. Before I had decided to "go general" in my discussions of Jonathan Edwards, I would spend the class period doing a paragraph by paragraph analysis of style and content. During one of these painfully dull sessions, I recall feeling personally offended when, upon looking up from my book (since I was really afraid of the class then—of eye contact—I spent much of the time looking down at my open book), I saw several of the students exchanging knowing glances. "What a turkey we have for a teacher!" was the interpretation I gave to their expressions. At another time I had indulged my sense of being personally hurt by stopping entirely the class proceedings and saying to the offending students (I think they were passing notes at the time), "This has got to stop. I just cannot put up with your insolence in this class any longer." It was a lie, of course. I would put up with their insolence because I lacked the will to take disciplinary action. I didn't want them to be mad at me. I wanted to be liked. I thought that a stern reprimand such as I had, in quavering voice, given, would fill them with chagrin at having hurt the feelings of their young teacher. "Poor guy! He's trying his best. Let's give him a break. Let's be constructive members of this class. Let each of us do his part in contributing constructively to our discussions. In that way we will be creating the proper atmosphere for enduring and important learning experiences!"

Such was the sort of fantasy which warped my mind at that time. When my dream vision was shattered by the apathy or open hostility of the students, I would begin to think of suitable hellish punishments for them. Several months after the above mentioned emotional scene I had the opportunity to wreak my revenge on one of the students who particularly enraged me in the senior class. I received a ballot for the election of the recipient of a local patriotic organization's award for patriotism, leadership, pleasantness, innocuousness, and so forth. This boy's name was on the ballot. I was tempted to vote against him out of spite but thought again about it and decided to refrain from voting at all out of my greater despisal of the organization presenting the dubious award.

I thought of this organization as the bastion of all the forces of Darkness and Nonthink which it was the mission of the educator to oppose. At that time it had not been clearly impressed upon me that a teacher was merely a servant to the community; I had also forgotten that those who were called educators in Athens were also slaves.

Gradually I learned not to react so personally to the dullness or hostility of the students. I began, in other words, to develop a consciousness of myself as an actor portraying a teacher, not of me being myself. I began to worry about whether certain remarks I was tempted to say would be in keeping with the characterization I was trying to present. How sarcastic should I be? How provocative on moral or political issues? How personal should I be with them, in regard to both myself and them? I found myself strongly tempted to treat my students as if they were my peers, not aware of the great gap which separated us—not of years, obviously, but of experience. With the attractive girls, and there were many, I found it difficult to resist the temptation to flirt, thus nourishing a new source of tension. At least one of their number found me to be an easy victim of her charms. Her actions will be the subject for further discussion later on.

So absorbed was I in the day-to-day crisis that it came as a great shock to me to discover, close to the end of the first grading period, that I really did not have much data upon which to base a fair evaluation of my students. Having been some six years removed from the high school environment myself, and having in the interim become accustomed to the mid-term exam, final exam, term-paper routine of college course work, I had not given much thought to the matter of tests and papers when I began to teach. More because of a desire to vary routine class activities than to discover the effectiveness of my teaching, I had given quizzes to the juniors on *Macbeth* and one or two short theme assignments to the seniors. I recall noting with some embarrassment the sparseness of little red marks in my grade book in comparison with the handsome display of the same in the grade books of other teachers. The end of the first grading period, consequently, was a very trying experience for me.

It was puzzling to me how experienced teachers could grade as much student work as their grade books indicated. I found it extremely difficult at first to grade just one theme. Just as I feared making students mad at me by taking disciplinary action, so I also feared their ire as a result of the low grades I might give them on papers and tests. I think I rationalized this scruple (if that is what it was) by saying to myself, "Who am I to judge the excellence of a student's work?" Obviously the consequence of carrying this sort of philosophy to various logical conclusions would be complete withdrawal from all evaluative activities—i.e., who am I to judge the worth of this presidential candidate; who am I to judge the sourness of this milk, etc. But at the time, that way of thinking had a definite appeal to my propensity for self-doubt.

Implied in what I have just said is the fact that my students were covertly manipulating me in this matter of grading. Like Neville Chamberlain, I saw the process as one of compromise, not of capitulation. Like Chamberlain, I was deceiving myself without deceiving the other side. I believe I also defended my lenience in grading with the reflection that generous grades would encourage rather than discourage the students to strive to attain excellence. I had heard somewhere that such positive reinforcements did indeed work. They did not work in my class. Seeing that they could do no worse than a C minus on even their dullest papers, and that they could fail to pass my "objective" tests only with the most strenuous effort, my students felt that they had been given a year's reprieve from conscientious work. Thus my generosity on the academic side reinforced my students' tendency toward inattentiveness caused by my lenience in disciplinary matters. It was not a pleasant experience to stand before such a class and ask to be respected.

The first grading period was a time of panic and expedient accommodation. As I have already indicated, I lacked the confidence in my own abilities to judge honestly the work of my students in some areas, and I lacked the experience to know what was a fair evaluative procedure and what was an unfair one. Sheepishly I submitted my strange distribution of grades to the department chairman. With the ritualistic precision of some priest of pedagogy, he brought forth a grade distribution chart which reminded his minions of the possible sins of commission in the form of excessive A's awarded to students in college preparatory (as distinguished from, and lower than, honors), courses. To me, in my most defensive sensitivity, it seemed that giving a student an A in one of my classes meant that that individual had been granted near-approval for a transfer up from the Purgatory of the preparatory class to the Heaven of honors, receiving there all the privileges and immunities attendant therein. Having given nine A's, I feared the wrath of the chairman. But he was lenient with my inexperience.

Grading period passed, and feeling that I had learned from the experience not to wait until the end of the semester to determine the worth of students, I resolved to give more attention to the assigning of papers and the construction of tests. My juniors had finished *Macbeth,* thank God, and would now be reading short stories; and these would be convenient, period-sized morsels easy for their intellectual digestion. The seniors had progressed into the 1840s, and would be encountering Thoreau and Emerson. I anticipated a series of ideological skirmishes below those two promontories.

Had I not just had a course in New England transcendentalists at the University of Chicago, I might have been as bored with the pomposity of Emerson as some of his co-transcenders were said to have become. Had I not been an avowed idealist, I would doubtless have been as scandalized at the thoughts and actions of Thoreau as Emerson apparently became. As it was, I was interested to see whether the students might be affected by my interest in the two authors—affected to such an extent that they might alter their own philosophies as a result of the experience.

Thoreau, more than Emerson, provoked the scorn of the seniors. Emerson could be dismissed as Edwards' ideas were dismissed: ethereal nonsense, irrelevant tripe, incomprehensible profundities. Thoreau, on the other hand, was writing about matters which had contemporary equivalents. Not even the dullest student could fail to sense the relatedness of "Civil Disobedience" to recent events. I asked the students to react in writing to some of the statements Thoreau was making in that tract. Did they agree or disagree with him on the issues he raised? What did they think of a person who preferred to obey his own instinctual sense of right and wrong instead of the laws of the state?

I think my prejudice in favor of Thoreau was quite obvious to them when the time came to justify the grades I had given on the themes they had turned in. Of course, their first complaint was that I could not possibly grade their work, because they were just expressing their opinions, and opinions could not be graded.

Recalling but not applying my "who am I to judge" standard, I was tempted to agree with them; but then I realized that such a capitulation would not be one which I could continuously maintain, so I informed the class that it was not the opinion that was being inspected for correctness or incorrectness; it was rather the manner and thoroughness with which the student presented that opinion and reinforced it with supporting arguments.

In our class discussion of the ideas contained in "Civil Disobedience" and the relevance of those ideas to the present, I found myself again falling into the *persona* of the righteous prosecutor. Once the transition had been made from the Mexican War to the Vietnam War, the class and I exchanged charge and countercharge with great fervor. They were not, of course, surprised to hear that I opposed that war. Neither were they very interested in listening to the reasons I gave for my opposition. Likewise, in my belligerence for the pacific cause I had put aside my toleration of their opinions in order to savor my contempt for their unenlightened right-wing outlook on the world. When they accused the draft card burners (to their way of thinking, a group of battalion strength) of being traitors, I suggested that some would say they were greater patriots than the soldiers who participated in an illegal and immoral war for the sake of their loyalty to their nation. I cited the resolutions regarding moral obligation made at Nuremberg following World War II, thereby slyly making guilty by association with Nazism those of my students who felt that obedience to established laws was the primary obligation of citizens. My zeal made me wonder whether the real reason I had decided to teach was to have a forum for the propagation of unpopular sentiments regarding morality, patriotism, and authority. I could not conceive of allowing the discussion of such issues to be carried on with me acting as an impassive moderator, and yet I did not like becoming such an impassioned spokesman for causes that lacked advocates in my classes. Such partisanship only reinforced the conviction the students had that, on top of being an easy touch in grading and discipline and a target for flirtation and flattery, I was so thoroughly off-beat politically and philosophically that my opinions could be dismissed as the amusing but innocuous rantings of a nut.

One day for some reason the seniors were paying less attention than usual to my gropings for discussion topics, and one of them suggested that I divulge my autobiography to them, as there were twenty minutes left in the period. I modestly obliged, relieved that someone had discovered an alternative to my frustrating attempts to move the class from minute to minute. I painted for them a picture of the horrible tribulations which college would no doubt be for them, full of onerous reading lists devoured in dimly lit libraries or crowded dormitories. The symptoms of student melancholia were described for them also, so that when they felt a bout of it coming on, they could appropriate preventative action, such as indulging in sleep, or liquor, or some other palliative. At this point I was pleased to see the wide-eyed look of wonder, so often found on the faces of toddlers listening to ghost stories, appear on the otherwise expressionless faces of the seniors.

Following the college segment I went on to relate to them my not very extensive or conclusive experiences among the Spokane Indians. They had about the same conception of the plight of the Indian as I had when I was in high school, and sensing this, I couched my comments to them in the terms of compassionate concern, with which they hearts harmoniously throbbed. VISTA had been my one indulgence in humanitarianism, and I had not been rewarded with the successes which I had foreseen. Because it had put much of my idealism in perspective, it had been an important experience for me. And because I wanted my students to think of me as Conrad's Marlow thought of Lord Jim—as "one of us"—I presented my experiences as a helpful barometer of the true course of idealism in the world of realists.

This baring of the real self to my seniors did not produce the desired results of honesty and authenticity. Instead, "The Further Adventures of Our English Teacher" became a serialized substitute for discussion whenever the opportunity presented itself in that class. A barrier had been broken between student and teacher, and several students thought that was just swell. After several days of this transgression, I found myself no longer in agreement.

As I mentioned previously, the juniors, after slugging through nine weeks of tedious, nebulous discussions concerning *Macbeth,* then went on to what I thought would be a somewhat easier consideration of short stories. Well, it was easier for a short while. At least it seemed that the change was appreciated by the class.

Then normality reasserted itself, and the junior classes were back in their old grooves. One class in particular could normally be counted upon for the production of horrors. Almost every day, I could count on being insulted or otherwise verbally abused as soon as I entered the room. One of the boys would delight in nasalizing my name in that distasteful Midwestern accent so offensive to one who, like myself, had been raised in the calmer phonetic patterns of Philadelphia. Another lad thought it amusing to play around with a veritable thesaurus of words which my name resembles in sound. If only he had been so clever in more important matters. Invariably, my lengthy answer to one student's question would provoke the commencement of a conversation by several other students in other parts of the room. Knowing that I might offend the interested student by breaking off my answer to her question to rebuke the inattentive ones, and also knowing that unless I enforced some control I would not be able to re-involve the other students in a continuation of the discussion which the interested student's question had, through my manipulation, thus far so nobly advanced, I found myself faced with a dilemma which I resolved feebly—neither choosing wholly one or the other alternative. In such a circumstance I became enraged at the disinterested ones, thinking of them as being snide, rude, sly, stupid, smug, twaddle-brained, pig-headed, Yahooish creatures whose senseless grins and looks of bovine contentment dispelled from my mind all belief in their claims to membership in the community of sensible human beings. It was pleasing to me to dismiss them in this way. But they seemed not to be willing to let me escape with my baser pleasures. It was not until the offenders had provoked me to an outburst of rage that they were placated and were willing to relent in their provocations. It was apparently entertaining for them to watch me shout my head off at them.

After classes in which such outbursts had occurred, I would retreat to the faculty cafeteria to repair my tattered ego. With stomach churning over a starch-loaded lunch of chicken à la king on rice with rolls and potato salad, I would tell myself that those students simply did not appreciate the fine and intelligent person that I was. Why on earth did I want to take myself and my work so seriously? They couldn't understand me even if they wanted to. I was so far above their heads that it would take years for them

to catch up with me. They were arrogant by nature and by domestic conditioning. I had seen their parents on Go To School night. I
could almost have placed the parent with the offspring on the
basis of the foolish grin of the elders corresponding to the foolish
grin of the younger ones. The attitude their expressions betrayed
that night were mirrored in the attitudes continually displayed in
my classes: "This guy is teaching my son. This guy thinks he's
something great. I never thought much of English. What a bunch
of junk—poetry and all that stuff. What an ass this guy is!" So at
least they seemed to be thinking. For all I know they may have
been floating through the evening enveloped in alcoholic eupho-
ria, and were merely registering that vague happiness in their
benign expressions. A defensive sensitivity, as I have before indicated, tends to see things differently.

I learned over a period of months that in order to survive in
the classroom I had to take on the *persona* of someone acting as a
teacher. That is, I had to shut down spontaneity and candidness
on my part and in their place put on a calculated facade of coolness and patience. Gradually I began to sound as if I had memorized a script. When I seemed to be acting as if I really knew what
I was doing and where I and the class were going, and when,
through the careful articulation of each utterance, accompanied
by the slow scanning of the entire classroom, I mesmerized the
students into the docility which overcomes alligators whose
tummies have been rubbed, then something like order would exist
and ideas might possibly have a chance of penetrating the thick
shields of dullness which encased their brains. Having noted this
phenomenon, I resolved to alter my methods by speaking always
in the manner I had when I first observed this effect. I found that
I could not. I found that when I did I would have a sparkling
vision of my old fourth grade teacher, the kindly Miss Richter,
and I would hear her dulcet voice speak to me as if oracular,
praising my way of speaking, and urging me to further articula-
tions in that manner. It was too much to ask of anyone.

This vision reminded me of a visit I had made to a high school
the previous year. The teacher whose class I observed spoke in
precisely the same way: in a slow, well-modulated, vocally con-
stipated, deliberately simple voice. Not only did his students
receive this diction, but also his colleagues, I noted, were addressed in this "I'll-speak-slowly-so-that-you-may-hear-every-

word-I-say" manner. This recollection, in addition to my re-membrance of a teacher from the past, made me glad that I could not sustain the language lab/airport paging-service voice for very long.

With the slow accretion of experience, I refined my thoughts on what one must do to his personality in order to be effective in the class. Instead of believing generally that one must become a sort of actor, I decided that, specifically, the sort of actor one should become was the Ronald Reagan variety. A Reaganesque egghead, a chalk-wielding charlatan, could more easily capture the minds and hearts of his students because his approach to them would be couched in the soothing terms of humility. "Shucks, you guys, I don't know what Whitman means any more than you do. But by gum, I sure as the dickens want to learn about him. We as Americans are obliged to know something about the fine and gallant gentlemen who made our country the showplace of the arts that it so manifestly is today."

It seemed to me that I became more effective as I became less genuine as an individual. When I had periodic lapses into my actual personality, I felt that these were invariably detrimental to me in my attempt to teach. They hurt me because they made me vulnerable to attempts by the students to fraternize. Fraterni-zation made objectivity difficult for me, and totally devastated my credibility as an enforcer of order in the class. Without some order in the class, obviously it would be hard for me to get the sort of concentration on learning which was necessary before learning was to take place.

If my remarks up to this point have seemed circular and repeti-tive in form, as if the same problem obsessed me throughout the year, appearing in slightly different forms as different circum-stances required, the reason is that this is indeed the way the year was for me. Constantly I felt the tension of an internal conflict between the way I knew I had to act as a teacher and the way I really wanted to act as a person. When a student acted in a way which was offensive to my teacher *persona,* I artificially felt offended but did not feel really offended. That was at first. Later I discovered that, whereas I could make the distinction between the two parts of my personality, my students had not that ability nor the interest to make this distinction. I learned that most stu-dents thought of me as a *unity,* not a *duality*—as "Mr. Cornog-

English-Teacher," not as Mr. Cornog/English Teacher. Thus I was being sort of a fool when I took ironic offense at offensive actions: those acts were directed against as much of the personal "me" as the students ever cared to become acquainted with. By showing not genuine, but rather feigned, anger when my authority had been challenged, I appeared to the students not to take myself seriously. Noting this, they felt, quite understandably, that they had no obligation to take me seriously either. And from this beginning developed the flourishing frustration of my first year.

Having obliquely apologized for the repetitiousness of my narrative, I will now ask for the further indulgence of my readers as I once more make the rounds of my classes. In some ways and on some days they were all invariably the same; in other ways nearly every day they were almost infinitely variable. Both fortunately and unfortunately, one of the invariable factors in each of the classes was the strong conflict of personalities existing between myself and one of the students. In my recollection of those conflicts and those students, I now smile at my awkwardness and their earnestness. I do not, however, dismiss as trivial or laughable the substantive matters over which we did psychological and ideological battle.

One of my junior English classes was principally the province of a short, skinny boy, named Brian. Clearly Brian did not like me. Perhaps he did not like anyone, but clearly he did not like me. Over a period of several months, Brian felt it was his duty to entertain the class with witty and slashing punctuations to our discussions. He found that wise cracks directed against me personally were the most amusing to the entire class, so he spent much time criticizing my appearance, my voice, or my idiosyncratic gestures. When I ignored him he would become displeased. He would continue his insults until they had drawn forth from me some indication that I was insulted. He obviously wanted recognition. He usually got it in the form of a detention, and he and I would spend a half-hour after school talking about his behavior and what could be done about it.

During these detention sessions, I would try to reason with Brian to make him see that I didn't dislike him personally but that his conduct certainly wasn't helping me run a very good class. At these sessions he had a consistent line about the rottenness of all teachers and schools and about his mission in the world being to make more miserable the lot of all adults associated with such institutions. I would call to his attention the fact that his disruptive behavior jeopardized the learning of other students through its tendency to cause me to halt proceedings and administer warnings and threats. He was not impressed by this argument, saying that that was just tough for them. Once or twice during our detention discussions I would ask Brian for some positive suggestions. He would respond by suggesting a total abandonment of the current curriculum and a transformation of the English class period into a study hall/play period. I persevered and asked him to give me one or two suggestions which I could consider for the next day's class. At this point it seemed that he was really trying to think of some way of improving the attitude he had, but he never did come up with a concrete suggestion.

The sad thing about our little discussions was that they so rarely got to the stage of serious probings of causes and effects of his hostility. I think that by the time he got to me, Brian had been conditioned by teachers and parents to be distrustful of teachers and parents. So it was that the effects of detention conversations had usually worn off before our next encounter in English. There he would be, smiling as a cat smiles at the mouse, ready with his first quip of the day. (It seemed at such times that he really needed me as a psychological fix of some sort. Without his daily shot of insults, Brian might have shrunk to mere normality in his conduct.) Without a target for verbal abuse (to speak more seriously), Brian might have had to find a more violent outlet for his anger.

Anger and hatred characterized much of what Brian said. At one time he thought I might be Jewish. Consequently he spent a week or more thinking of scornful things to say about Jews. Then he dropped that line of attack and became violently anti-Catholic, thinking perhaps that that was my religion. If I did not react to his taunts in a reasonable period of time, he would take more drastic action. He would move his desk about the room. When I asked him why he was doing that, he would say he wanted to get away from some student because that person offended him. I would tell him to move his chair back, and he would. Then, while I was writing something on the board or talking to a student in another part of the room, he would move his chair inch by inch back to the unacceptable spot. When I became angry with him for doing this and shouted, the class would be amused and he would have scored a triumph over my coolness. "You're losing control of yourself, Mr. Cornog. Boy, are you getting red in the face!" He would be right, but somehow I received no consolation from this fact.

In class one day I repeated the line I had given to Brian earlier in one of our detention sessions: "I don't care if you dislike me personally; it's what I stand for that you should respect." That day I was feeling particularly collected and imperturbable. I spoke the line as if I really meant it. At the time, I probably thought I did mean it (my inconsistency again showing itself), but now I don't think that I feel that way. I care very much if a student despises me personally. It hurts to be hated. I want everyone to know what a swell and great person I really am. That's one of the reasons I'm in teaching—ego gratification: I want to show people how smart I am. It is especially painful, when I have made an effort to show the students what my real feelings are about something, to hear them treat my thoughts with scorn.

It finally occurred to me that more often than not their apathy and hostility were not directed really at me as a person, but at me in the capacity of a teacher. What I had translated into *ad hominem* thrusts at me were actually no more than manifestations of students' general dislike for English and school. Because I was a novice, I couldn't separate myself from what I taught. Cold objectivity had yet to cloak me in its protective and distancing shield.

I have described the sort of tension which existed between Brian and myself, but I don't think I've named it directly. It was a conflict caused by my desire to have Brian see that he was in error in his assessment of my personality. He was unfairly making a fool of me in front of the class; he was maliciously distorting me for the purpose of amusing his fellow students and gratifying his own sense of self-esteem. I felt that the respect which I so greatly needed would never be allowed to surface unless the submerging quality of Brian's jests could be tempered. In my other classes I did not detect such an overt lack of respect. I did, however, find abundant sources for tension and conflict.

In one class there dwelt a fair young creature who found me to be an easily flustered appreciator of her many charms. She was a coquette and, to my way of thinking, a dangerous one. She had me at a great disadvantage. While she could liltingly ask

special favors of me (such as my continued toleration of her misbehavior in class), I could not cope with her in anything like a
spontaneous way. Unless I was in a phenomenally commanding
mood, I could expect to hear such daily entreaties as "Oh, Mr.
Cornog! Mr. Cornog! Could you come here and help me?" "Mr.
Cornog, I just don't understand!" (All this spoken in a voice of
tender urgency.) She would have her left arm raised, her right
arm aiding it, and would be leaning forward and upward from
her desk so that (I thought) I would not fail to notice her finer
endowments (I didn't).

"What is it, Julie?" I would reply, hoping the fear in my heart
would not be evident in my voice. It nearly always was.

"Mr. Cornog, there's something here I don't understand. Could
you come here and look at it?"

Don't, I tell myself. *Don't.*

"Read it to me and I'll explain it." (*From here,* I almost added,
but that would be too obvious.) No. She's getting up.

"I'll bring it up there."

She approaches. She arrives at my left side. I note a scent of
lemony perfume; an attempt at make-up about the eyes. She
leans over to place the book in front of me, and some of her long
dark hair grazes my shoulder. By this time I feel thoroughly unwilling to answer any question regarding syntax. *What about
private tutoring?* I hear my lecherous innards suggesting. Heaven
forbid! My frustration causes me to blurt a response to her query,
hoping that she'll return to her seat. The class by this time has
observed me melting into a limpid pool behind the desk. She must
be smiling triumphantly above me, her glory reflected in my
devastation. If only she had been as innocent of malice in her
manipulations as I had been tender in my innocence, then all
would have been well. Alas, she was not. She thought it great
sport to exercise her arts for the benefit of her friends, and I
could think of no way to break the spell. I could not ignore her,
because then the class would notice my attempt and think that
she had really gotten to me. I could not allow her to continue to
dominate me, for then the respect I sought would never appear.
Who could respect a hen-pecked English teacher? The befuddled
teacher doing battle with the temptress every day—what a tab-
leau! What a cliché. It pained me to see myself in such a humiliating posture. It was so absurd.

Another of my problem students was Jack, the school's star

athlete. Beneath our surface appearance of mutual respect and toleration, Jack and I had really a rather strong dislike for each other. When we were involved in a discussion about some matter of values, he would seem to speak earnestly and pleasantly, as if he were really interested in our discussion and thought such discussions were of some importance. Then when I turned away from him I would notice his expression change to one which seemed to say, "He actually took me seriously! I was just putting him on!" He ridiculed me behind my back.

Jack and I represented different life-styles. He valued physical prowess and dexterity, I their mental equivalents. He fancied himself a realist and thought practicality a superior approach to life than my idealism. I categorized his way of thinking under the heading, "Jock-mentality." I don't know what category he put me in. Our year in English will be remembered by me as a long series of incomplete or oblique confrontations between our two incompatible philosophies. Our mutual contempt was never very far below the surface of our actions.

It seemed to me at the time that it was entirely appropriate that we should feel the way we did, given the nature of the literature we read. As I have already pointed out, the seniors and I early discovered that we would not be able to get along when certain issues presented themselves for discussion. The anti-intellectualism (there we are, another category) of which Jack was guilty was just another name for the attitude of those Americans so dazzled and awed by the myth of the American Dream of material well-being that they consider immaterial concerns un-American. Jack was simply an American dreamer. For him success was to be measured by visible calibrations, not invisible cerebrations: how much did you earn, where did you live, for which corporation did you work—these were the important questions, not what did you think about this book or that lecture. During a class in which a "let's be perfectly frank" mood prevailed, Jack confided, "You know, with your brains and your ability and your education, you could be making three times what they're paying you to teach. So why do you teach?" Couched in those terms, revealing as they did a mentality hard for me to understand, difficult for me to accept, the question was nearly unanswerable.

There was this strange thing about Jack: As I've said, he could seem to be "playing your game" up to a point—he could accept

for purposes of pleasing a teacher certain assumptions about what is important and what is unimportant; but when I tried to discuss "relevant" issues with the class, he would quickly forget the existence of any value system except his own, and would filter all considerations through the cloaca of his material mind.

Relevant issues—here is where two important currents of my experience converged. Vietnam, race relations, violence in American life—these were the issues that were constantly in the background of our discussions of American literature in the senior class. Previously I mentioned the way in which a discussion of Thoreau turned into a discussion of Vietnam and the matter of draft resistance. I mentioned also my somewhat conceited self-analogization with *Lord Jim*—my wish that my students see me as "one of them." Generally what this meant to me was that my students would be made aware of a point of view different from but just as credible as the one their parents had been presenting to them. Having been raised in a suburban environment similar to theirs, and having attained the Ivy League education to which (I thought) they all aspired, I thought my divergent opinions might be seen as acceptable for the reason that their expounder was sort of a "soul brother." Coordinate with this was my wish that my students see me as a *momento maturitatis:* "As I am now, you are now becoming." This, too, I hoped, would influence the students not to dismiss as outlandish what I had to say, but rather to tolerate my ideas under the rule, "Maybe when I'm his age, I'll think the same way he does."

Thinking thus wishfully, I had forgotten to consider the overruling power of irrationality as a reinforcer of prejudice. Thus it was frustrating to me to hear Jack and the other like-minded students parrot stale opinions regarding patriotism when the war was discussed, or regarding "those people" when racial matters were mentioned. And it was shocking to me to see that not even the assassination of Martin Luther King shook them from their indifference.

That Friday after King's death I expected to devote my classes to a discussion of the man's life and the possible consequences of his death. I had in fact expected my students to initiate the discussion. This did not happen. It was as if nothing at all had taken place about which they should be upset. As the day progressed, I began to wonder whether they had heard of King's death—perhaps *I* had dreamed the whole thing. To me it was incredible that anyone could smile or be cheerful when there was so depressing a fact as that assassination present to be dealt with. By the time I met my seniors, I was determined not to tolerate our accepted routine—I was going to challenge them to confront King's death and feel it as a tragedy.

I brought the subject up; none of my seniors wanted to discuss it. I wanted to know what they knew about King. Most of them thought he was a good man. Most of them also felt he was a dangerous man who was threatening to them. They did not like what he stood for; they thought they had no obligation to consider Negroes as their equals; they felt that the burden of proof was on Negro shoulders: when they acted in an acceptable way, then they could receive the respect of whites. Out came the judgments: Negroes were lazy; they were treacherous; all Negro women did was have babies so that they could get more money from Aid to Dependent Children; all Negro men did was take that money and buy heroin and liquor. And so on. We talked about the possible relevance of King for suburb dwellers. Some of them, while prefacing their remarks with "I'm not prejudiced, but—" went on to tell me that Negroes really did lower property values, and that there were sound reasons for encouraging them to "stay with their own kind."

A few students—two, actually—were co-advocates with me of the cause for which King died. They and I knew that King was thought of as irrelevant by the more militant blacks. Together we tried to convince the rest of the class that King was moderate in comparison to these others—that they had lost a comparative friend and were faced now with more hostile leaders. It seemed that they couldn't see the distinction or realize the difference between King and the more militant leaders. They would rather believe that nonviolence was "all talk," that King was merely a puppet being manipulated by (a) communists or (b) black nationalists, for all sorts of immoral, illegal, and subversive purposes.

After class I recall feeling sick and weak and bitter. It was thoroughly depressing to see the lack of influence literature and I had had on those students. For them there was no connection between literature and life, or between the classroom and the outside world. I was not thinking of any novel in particular, but only of the moral values present in literature. Surely one of the great educative values of literature is that it makes a person more sensitive to the worth of individuals. I had hoped that it would not be impossible for students to see that Martin Luther King was a worthy man deserving of their respect. Was that so difficult for them? Couldn't they make the effort to judge the man by what he said and did, not by what he never said and never did? Would they never be touched by tragedy or affected by calamity? Did they always have to succumb to condemnation rather than aspire to understanding? I wondered. And I worried. It seemed to me that King's assassination was a test of my teaching and of all education—a test that I and my students had failed. It appeared to me that no learning was done in schools, really, but rather that schools were frivolous exercises indulged in by posturing pedants, "doing their things." It was like a nightmare in a way. With King's assassination came the opportunity to point and say: "This is it. This is the calculus which tells me how far you have been humanized by the humanities. Do you feel anything now, or are you as numb and indifferent as you have always seemed?" And, numbly indifferent, they would turn to each other and smile and wink and say, "What's he trying to prove?" It was enough to make one feel apologetic. "Pardon me, students, for bringing something real into the classroom, but—" But they did not pardon me. They condemned me to listen to their correction of my sadly misinformed ideas about King. "You've got it all wrong," they as much as said. "Who's been filling your mind with those lies?" Like a character in a Kafka story, I was so impressed by the rocklike firmness of their attitude that I began to wonder whether maybe they were right and I was wrong.

The remainder of the year was completed in a more serious manner than it had begun. I attempted artificially to induce understanding in my seniors by having them write narratives in which they were to describe how they might see life if they lived in an urban ghetto. To some extent this did require them to be more compassionate than they might otherwise have been. But still I sensed an attitude which said, "I can afford to be compassionate in writing. I will not be compassionate in what I say or how I act. That's something entirely different. This is make-believe; that's real-life." Earlier in the semester I would have been offended by this attitude; now I accepted it as the best I could get, given the circumstance of ingrained prejudice with which I had to work. At least, I thought, the students were being asked to consider a way of life far different from their own—a way of life that might have been their reality, save only for chance.

Along with the sobriety of the closing weeks went an unarticulated but nearly joyful anticipation of release from the contemptuous familiarity our months of togetherness had fostered in students and teacher alike. I shed not a tear at the prospect of never facing my students again; they no doubt were crossing the days off their calendars which separated them from liberation from my moralizings. I was grateful to them for serving as my initiators into the reality of teaching; they were grateful that that initiation was now at an end. It was far from Mr. Chips-ville in my classes when the last day came. One class ended in final disaster and chaos. A girl whom I had told two days before *not* to bring a beach ball to class brought a dozen. At a prearranged signal (how do students prearrange these things?) a dozen beach balls were suddenly being inflated before my uncomprehending eyes. Had not uproarious laughter thwarted the inflations, these balls were to have been launched jointly in my direction at some other prearranged signal like "Kill the teacher!"

Another class whimpered into extinction as I and the temptress parted company. I was greatly relieved at this, hoping that the experience had taught me something about how not to deal with coquettes in the classroom.

My senior class and I went our separate ways some days before due to the special arrangements made for seniors—graduation and all that ritualistic nonsense. Our last days were spent taking exams, so that classes tapered off rather than culminating in some cataclysmic finale of rancor and unpleasantness.

Had I a systematic, well-ordered mind, I would at this point summarize what I learned during my first year of teaching and leave my readers with explicit *caveats* which, if heeded, would steer them away from the quicksand into which so manfully, and so blindly, I strode. But such is not the case. I have not so much *learned* anything as I have been conditioned by a continuous repetition of experiences. The obvious reference is to Pavlov. Whereas before, when the word "teacher" was mentioned, my ears would not prick up, nor would my mouth salivate with the expectation of food, now they do. I don't know how instructive or conclusive this phenomenon is, really. All I know is, now I'm "one of them."

John Canfield

White Teacher, Black School

After four years of college, I still didn't know what I wanted to do, but I had to hurry up and make a decision or Uncle Sam was going to decide for me. It seemed that the easiest route was to become a majority statistic and join the 72.8 percent of my classmates in graduate school. The question was, studying what?

Law school was definitely out. As an undergraduate I had sold refrigerators at the law school. My brief encounter there convinced me that I didn't want to spend the next three years of my life in a cubicle memorizing thousands of names, dates, and cases. Besides, I had slept through the law boards.

Medical school had been eliminated by my freshman year when I got a C in introductory biology. Somehow I had failed to respond with the proper awe when I had finally managed to wrap a strand of DNA around the glass rod. Business school was— well, my father was in business as a salesman, and I—let's just say that I knew I didn't want to go into business.

There was always the Ph.D. route in my major—Chinese history! But after reading the requirements—a mastery of Chinese, Japanese, and a major European language; a master's paper, course work, a dissertation, and orals—well, let's face it. I had barely passed French my freshman year. All the missionaries to China had been written about, and I was growing weary of rice. More importantly, I guess, I had looked at my library of over five hundred books with all their important facts carefully underlined and carefully forgotten, and I realized that I was simply no longer interested in what I had spent the last four years studying.

The road to academic achievement was looking rather bleak until I administered a do-it-yourself aptitude test. I began by asking myself what I liked to do. What was I good at? The answer was that I liked people and I liked talking. I was curious about why people did things and I wanted to understand what made them tick. I also liked sports. I had always been in something: football, rugby, swimming, track. I liked kids, too. I suppose I had discovered this during the summers I had worked as a swimming instructor at a camp in Maine and the times I had spent just goofing around with my younger brothers and sister and their collection of friends. All of this was made easier, I'm sure, by the fact that I was still pretty much of a kid myself.

For the first time, I began to talk things over with my roommate, who had already made up his mind to go into education. The prospect of teaching began to seem so logical. I began to envision myself teaching in an Eastern prep school where I would be the big brother, the friendly but scholarly mentor. I'd hold bull sessions in my room, chaperone at all the dances, and maybe even help coach the football team. That seemed like a perfectly acceptable self-image for a Harvard graduate.

After taking a lot of tests, sweating out several interviews, and writing seven different versions of what I wanted to do with my life for seven different schools, I ended up at the Graduate School of Education at the University of Chicago. The year at the university was a kaleidoscope of seemingly unconnected events. There were courses to be digested; books to be read; papers to be written; theories to be contemplated, rejected, reworked, and accepted; and most importantly of all, strategies to be planned for the forthcoming year. It was here that I was confronted with Major Decision Number Two—where would I teach, once the course-work was completed. Actually, that decision had been evolving all year, and I hadn't realized it.

During the first few weeks of the master of arts in teaching (MAT) program we had been bussed to several schools in the city and the suburbs to make observations. The first school that we visited was Duncan High School. Later I learned that Duncan was nationally famous as a problem school of the "inner-city." It was one hundred percent black and situated in the heart of the city's ghetto.

Here I was, the typical middle-class white, who for the first time in his life was in a building where there were more Afro-Americans than whites. The visit was a confusing mélange of exciting, depressing, shocking, and relieving revelations. As I reluctantly left the school, I had mixed feelings. One feeling was that it was not as bad as the blackboard jungle I had seen in the movies. But at the same time there was a feeling of emptiness and depression from my wanting to stay and help in what seemed to be a futile battle against overwhelming apathy and ignorance—on the part of both the students and the teachers.

The next day we observed a plush suburban school. Everything seemed so new and bright—even the kids. Here in the land of well-trimmed lawns and spacious houses our group of forty were each given an expensive departmental syllabus and a banquet luncheon, while back at Duncan an overcrowded class in a dimly lit room was being told that they could not be issued textbooks to take home and read. The administration was sure that they would not be read, but merely lost and destroyed.

Later that same year a few of us in the social studies program went out to another city high school. The school had been an all-Negro school until its recent integration by a single white girl, the daughter of a minister working in the ghetto.

Thirty years ago this had been one of the status schools in the Chicago system. It was located in the center of a rich Jewish neighborhood. However, after the black migration from the South and the concomitant race to the suburbs and to the "Gold Coast" on the North Shore, the school joined that distinguished club known as the "inner city."

Upon arriving at the school and parking in the teacher's lot (one is told that he should always park in the lots if he values his hubcaps and bucket seats, because the lots are guarded) we went through the usual protocol of informing the principal who we were, and were granted visitors' passes. We were then escorted by a colonel in the ROTC (a girl) to the man we had come to see.

Mr. Seven is the head of the history department, and we had come to see him about the development of a course in community civics for ghetto children. After a tour of the physical plant, we settled down into the windowless textbook room to let Mr. Seven explain his department to us. Little by little he began to unveil the difficulties and realities of the urban school. For over an hour he continued to disillusion us with the facts of ghetto schools. Paper, which had been so cheap and abundant at the University of Chicago Laboratory School, was looked upon as a rare commodity here. The reproduction of materials was also a major problem since everything had to be approved by the central office. New books were reviewed and approved every third year in order to save the taxpayers' money. It seemed that the child attending such a school was doomed to be three years behind in the latest educational innovations. I was later to learn that even that state would be a utopian dream.

After meeting with the head of the department, we observed two classes. The first, taught by Mr. Jonas, was engaged in drawing fifteen maps (rainfall, population, etc.) of North America. While the students were working, we talked to Mr. Jonas. He was twenty-seven and was taking night courses for his master's degree. During the discussion we learned that he was an "FTB" or full-time-basis substitute. To be an assigned teacher, one has to pass an examination in his field and in education, then pass an oral exam. After this he can be permanently assigned to one school. Three years later he can obtain tenure. Mr. Jonas explained that an FTB could be transferred at any time without prior notice, that he received less pay, and that he was "used" by the system. We later learned that nearly fifty percent of the staffs of all inner city schools were FTB's.

During the class we asked the kids if they knew why they had to draw maps. They didn't. We asked them if they thought they were learning anything. They didn't. One girl did reassure us that it was fun to draw maps! As we carried on our little survey, we observed that the kids hardly ever talked above a low moan. Where was all the noise we had heard in the lunchroom? Why were they now so withdrawn? This was a very disturbing question.

The second class we observed was taught by an older man who had grown up in Iowa. He reminded me of the typical grandfather in every television series. He made us welcome and informed us that he used the discussion system.

It was certainly an interesting "discussion." He sat at his desk in the front of the room and asked: "What's hoof-and-mouth disease?" and other meaningful things. He almost got a discussion going in spite of himself when he asked what the difference was between the North and the South. He was trying to elicit the difference between an agricultural and industrial economy, but he received an answer having to do with racial prejudice. He ended that by trying to convince the kids that there was little racial prejudice in the North. The kids probably didn't believe him anyway, but they were being duped—not insidiously—by a presumably insensitive and naïve teacher.

As we left the building there were three policemen at the doorway talking to the principal. I couldn't decide whether they thought they were keeping the evil out or knew that they were keeping it in. I no longer felt I could teach in that prep school back East. I was needed here. Here was the challenge. Here was a system full of incompetency, irrelevancy, inanity, hypocrisy, inhumanity, and ignorance. Somehow I felt that I could and should help to remedy the situation by getting into the school system and bugging everyone with my flawless logic as to why they were wrong. Joining with the kids, who I believed to be my allies, we would subvert the system and bring about the revolution. Here I was, Don Quixote de la Mancha, mounted on my white steed, about to ride off into the ghetto with a copy of *Summerhill* under my arm.

September found me marching into Churchill High School ready to do battle. The first day was similar to an all-day teachers' meeting. There were no classes. Instead, the day started with a stark example of the reality of the job. We spent one hour taking IBM sheets, tearing them into separate stacks for the counselor's office, the main office, two for the program office, one for the student, and one for our files. Fun and games!

After this pleasant chore was over, we were treated to a presentation for the new teachers. Surprisingly there were quite a few of us. My first impressions were mostly favorable. There were a few who asked dumb questions, but the majority seemed eager and idealistic.

The administration proved to be more disappointing. The principal was more nervous than any of the new teachers. He wandered on and on in a solicitous attempt to be friendly and to assure us that we were all partners in "the exciting adventure of educating today's youth." It was all pretty corny, and the majority of the new teachers, being young, black, and hip, were turned off. After this introduction we had a condescending lesson on how to fill out the trillions of forms which someone somewhere had ingeniously invented. Then came the parade of assistant principals, librarians, counselors, and clerks, all of whom had to be introduced and accorded the right to extol the virtues of the school and the importance of their office in its proper functioning. I couldn't believe all the paperwork that was required (in duplicate, if you please). Most of it was related to the home room. There were a thousand forms to be passed out, to be filled, to be passed to the student to be filled out, or simply to be read aloud. Later in the year one got the feeling that they all should be thrown out.

The first day of real school was a bookkeeper's nightmare. There were absence reports, homeroom size reports, class size records, tardy slips, and cut slips to be passed out; and there were three schedule cards per student to be passed out, filled out, returned, and filed. Then there were parents' voter registration cards to be collected to prove that the students lived within the school district. Half the students didn't have these, and even if they had, I wouldn't have known which addresses were in the district anyway. Add to this the physical and dental exam forms to be collected, the bus cards to be filled out, lockers to be assigned, and the locks to be sold.

Lockers! For thirty-eight students I was assigned sixteen lockers, twelve of which worked. Therefore, kids had to double and triple up. Girls didn't want to be in with boys; friends wanted to be together; and one boy who was emotionally disturbed and uncoordinated could not work a combination lock. Each lock sold for $1.25, and I quickly learned that 2 and 3 do not divide equally into $1.25.

Three weeks later I finally achieved some semblance of secretarial order. I had meticulously entered names onto lines, placed IBM numbers into boxes, corrected misspellings, copied down new locker numbers, student numbers, and addresses, and placed on file the names of new locker partners acquired during the week and new fathers acquired over the summer. For one girl I had three addresses, two phone numbers, and three last names—all had to be entered on her records.

Financially, I was not as successful in dealing with the students. In addition to the locks there were fees to be collected: department fees, activity fees, and book money. The ten minutes allotted for homeroom always left me with five dollars and four names, but I quickly learned not to ask who had paid yesterday. If I did, thirty-eight hands were sure to shoot into the air in unison. On the first day I was advised by one of the teachers to take anything—even 10 cents on a dollar—because I'd be lucky to get that. I also learned to carry at least $2.00 worth of change at all times. It provided me with an instant reply to "But I've only got a dollar." This habit also earned me the undying friendship of the penny-pitching crowd.

That first day was chaos. All the freshman homeroom teachers were to meet their students in the lunch room before adjourning to permanent homerooms. Walking around for ten minutes with a sign that said "Homeroom 105," I located thirty-four of the thirty-eight on my roster. After having them write down their names to determine which thirty-four I had, I lined them up to take them to room 241. When we arrived, we were thirty-two. In my first task I had lost two kids. In a moment of prophetic reflection I quietly wondered how many more I would lose over the year. Those two finally showed up the next day, but the thought has never left me.

I was snapped out of this private world by the arrival of two seniors who were to be the "big brother" and "big sister" of my homeroom. After I introduced them to the class, I began to read out the list of school rules. I prefaced the whole thing by saying that I personally didn't like rules, but that that didn't exempt students from knowing them for their own protection. As I was reading the rules, the two seniors began to smile. This made me uneasy, for I so much wanted to avoid falling into the traditional teacher bag of being irrelevant to the existing reality. I decided that the next day I would let the big brother and sister do the talking. Maybe I would learn what the real scene was by watching.

After homeroom ended, I had to move down the hall to my first class. This was a more scary prospect, for it was not all meaningless red tape. Here was the confrontation, the real thing. Here was where learning was supposed to take place. Suddenly I wished for a form to hand out to cover my uncertainty. But I managed to make it through the forty minutes with only one unsettling event.

Having carefully pronounced all the names on the attendance list, I had launched into my rehearsed speech about what we would hopefully be doing for the rest of the year. As I was finally beginning to relax (I think I was actually expecting someone to throw a rotten tomato at me if my performance were bad), the door opened—no knock—and a very attractive elderly woman led two students into the room. As the two girls began to feel their way to a desk, I suddenly realized they were blind. Wow! "What do I do now?" I thought. But there wasn't time to think about that. The period was almost over and I had hardly plowed through the first half of my speech. At the end of the class I volunteered two students to take the girls to their next class, and rushed off to find post number two on the second floor. That was where I was supposed to be hall guard.

Hall duty was an enlightening experience. It brought me face to face with myself as an agent of the school, a role which I would fight for the remainder of the year. Here I was Joe Policeman. I was to keep the halls clear and quiet, apprehend thieves breaking into lockers, and reroute errant wanderers to their destinations. At first this seemed easy enough. I simply walked around and my mere presence seemed to hurry people on their way. But it was not long before I saw a problem. It appeared in the form of four boys descending the stairs, sounding like a rhythm and blues record. I hesitated. I knew all this noise had to be wrong, but I liked their sound. It was really good. If I said, "All right, that'll be enough of that," it seemed I would be untrue to myself. I had nothing against their singing. In fact, it was really a welcome relief to the preceding two hours. But I did have to do something, so I tried to tell it like it was. I said, "Look, man, I really dig your sound, but I'm afraid it's going to get all five of us in trouble. So why don't you rehearse somewhere else?"

Their response was a simple, "OK, man" and off they went. In this brief encounter I had profoundly realized that I could not be the archetypal authoritarian teacher carting off students to see the assistant principal. Somehow I couldn't, and still can't, relate to people through a role such as teacher to student. That just was not my way. If I couldn't relate to people on a person-to-person basis, I couldn't do it at all.

While I was still on hall duty, my department chairman approached me and said, "You're creating quite a bit of commotion, you know."

"I assume you mean my beard," I said.

"That's right," he answered. "Now personally I don't care.

I think a person has the right to decide for himself whether or not he wants to wear a beard. The principal, as usual, probably won't take a position on it, but the problem is Miss Middy, the disciplinarian. She feels it will cause trouble when she has to tell some of the kids who have grown mustaches over the summer to shave." He went on to say that he felt teachers, as adults, had certain rights which children did not have, thereby giving support to me. I felt, on the other hand, that if they didn't bother the few kids who had the mustaches, they could avoid a problem by not creating one. I had always been a proponent of students' rights, and I could now see that the front office and I were going to have an ideological conflict. How much of a split, and to what degree, I could never have predicted. But that was to come later.

During the first few weeks I was too busy trying to work with the students in my classes to think much about the crisis which would come later. There were lessons to prepare, books to read, new textbooks to assimilate, papers to grade, materials to reproduce, and most importantly, names to connect with faces—130 of them plus an additional 117 teachers.

My main goal for the first few weeks, however, was to establish some kind of rapport with the students, to create the atmosphere that I felt was conducive to creative learning. I told them that traditional history was out, that the text book was boring, often wrong, and certainly discriminatory in its omission of important Negro history. I tried to make them understand that we would not look at history as a bunch of facts to be memorized, but as a key to understanding the seemingly chaotic present.

I believe I got through to them with this message. Most of their educational lives, teachers had been shoving irrelevant textbook knowledge down their throats. Then here comes me, on the first day agreeing with them that textbooks and school are mostly a bore. They could hardly do anything but agree with me. Perhaps we could begin to try to remedy that situation together.

We spent the first couple of weeks developing some theories about the problems of modern society: premarital sex, alcoholism, organized crime, drugs, racial strife, poverty, the war, big business, and the draft. These topics evoked some enthusiastic participation from almost everybody. The students wrote papers about their own experiences and thoughts, conducted a community survey on a controversial topic, and engaged in pretty spirited discussions.

I remember feeling happy when I overheard one of my students as he entered class remark to a classmate, "OK, let's have another lively discussion today." During that particular class we continued a discussion we were having on Black Power. After everyone had aired his views, I outlined how we would look at men like Nat Turner, W. E. B. Dubois, Marcus Garvey, Wallace D. Fard, and Noble Drew Ali to find historical roots of the present movement. The two white kids in the class did not seem caught up in the same spirit as the rest of the class. One of them, the girl, approached my desk after class. I was expecting her to say something like, "Are we going to spend all of our time talking about Negroes?" What she did say was, "Mr. Canfield, there's one thing you should know. I'm hard of hearing. You'll have to talk louder so I can hear you." What a shock! She had hardly heard a word that had been said. So I agreed to write more on the blackboard and lend her my class notes.

Another of the unsettling realizations during the first days in the classroom was that my eyes kept falling on certain faces: the green-eyed girl in the middle row, the girl in the back who finally looked up from her comic book or the letter she's writing to her friend in the front of the room, the Greek kid who looked like Tony Curtis, the boy who kept cracking jokes (ones even I had to admit were funny), and the girl in the mini-skirt who looked twenty—in general, the bright and the good looking. But what of the others: the tall boy with acne and glasses, the fat girl who really turned me off, the short kid with the birthmark on his face, the cheap-looking girl with the ratted hair—the common everyday kid in the class? So I began to try to look at all of them; I felt guilty. All those ed. psych. lectures came back: "Look at the kids . . . make 'em feel important . . . reinforce them," but, damn it, I keep seeing that girl in the middle row. Even she began to put her head down when I'd look at her. "Is she embarrassed? Good God, Jack, she'll think you're a dirty old man. Look away! The Lolita complex has come out of hibernation."

The same thing happens with names; right off you know at least half of them—the girl in the middle row, the Greek kid, the joker. But what about the other half? I didn't want to make them sit in fixed seats, for that would place restrictions on the freedom I was trying to create and rigidify the atmosphere of the classroom. But by the end of the first week you're embarrassed not to know their names. So you do things like putting all the papers of the kids whose names you don't know on the top so that when you hand them out, the names will stick in your mind. You use all kinds of tricks because you've got to know that name. Watching a kid's face light up when you use his name or when you say, "Well, as Larry said earlier . . . ," you know it's worth it.

One of the major things I remember from the first weeks of teaching was the constant interruptions. There were people bearing messages, special bulletins and requests for students from the counselors' office; there were tardy students with passes from everyone in school except the janitors; there were teachers in search of chalk, erasers, absence slips, and books; and still more students looking for their tablets, purses, and tennis shoes left behind the period before. One of the least pleasant but often repeated interruptions was the girl from the main office bearing a slip which read, "Please report to room _____ period _____ to substitute for _____." Not a hell of a lot one can do. The union rules say you don't have to teach during your free period, but unfortunately one has to eat lunch in the same room as the administration, and who wants to get indigestion? I had already been told that my beard had caused some of the older women to lose their appetites. "Fine," was my first reaction. "Maybe they'll die of malnutrition and be replaced." The division between older and younger teachers was already taking place. But one didn't need the office help against him also.

Whenever I substituted, I tried to improvise some kind of relevant lesson rather than just sit at the desk and keep order. The reason for this was that some classes never had a regular teacher. I was trying to fill this void with some learning. The first time I substituted was in an English class. That day I decided to initiate a discussion about the use of words and their meanings. When I entered the class I wrote the words "riot" and "rebellion" on the blackboard, and then asked what the difference was between the two in relation to last summer's conflagrations in Newark and Detroit. The class handled that pretty well, but really got up tight when I tried to get them to think about the words, "Negro," "Afro-American," "Afro-Asian," and "Black." They just did not want to get involved in it. The girls, it appeared, wanted to be referred to as "Negro," and the boys as "Afro-American." I think the difference lay in the nature of their aspirations. Most of the girls at the school are very middle class in their attitudes and wear the latest in preppy and mod fashions; the guys, on the other hand, didn't seem so positive or optimistic as the girls about their future. The boys just seemed to be bitter about what they didn't have. One gets the impression that the girls want to emulate success, and hopefully someday marry it. The boys have a different idea about how to get it, or just have a "screw-it-all-anyway" attitude. This same phenomenon manifested itself in the clubs within the school. A quick scanning of the membership lists shows that they are filled predominantly with females. The Junior and National Honor Societies are extreme examples.

The other thing to emanate from these sessions was the realization that the students were ignorant of their own heritage and their social predicament. Many had been sheltered from the grossest forms of prejudice by affluent and loving parents, nice homes, and similarly situated friends. I remember one boy who was sure that black people outnumbered whites in America. He had never been out of the ghetto in his entire sixteen years. The civil rights movement seemed far removed from their thoughts, and their history was virtually unknown to them. They'd never heard of the Mississippi Freedom Democratic Party, Frederick Douglass, Senator Brooke, or Adam Clayton Powell. But that's what I was here for: to educate, to awaken, to create awareness. I had read that one becomes alienated from the present if he doesn't know his past. In their past, then, could be found pride of race and understanding of the present. That would have to be one of my goals for the year.

In addition to black history I wanted them to understand the main forces at work in American society and their relation to them. The other focus would be skills: the ability to read, write, speak, analyze, and reason effectively. I wanted my students to leave my classes with a new-found confidence in their own abilities, potentials, and achievement.

After growing to know and love thirty people in a class, you ache with anxiety for their success. That's true with any friendship, I guess, for with it comes a deep concern and responsibility.

One is constantly lending them money, recommending books, taking them to conferences, getting them out of trouble, helping them apply to college, talking them out of loafing, giving them second, third, and fourth chances, and most importantly, listening, listening, listening, and only then offering advice.

Every minute I taught in the classroom, and as I walked through the halls, and met kids on the street, I wondered if I were being accepted, if they thought I was real. I suppose that this was one of the biggest hangups I had in my first year of teaching. Being young and single, I guess I was driven by a desire or a need to be loved and accepted by those with whom I was in daily contact. I am sure that in some measure I was also driven to be accepted by what black militants would term my own inadequacies and guilt feelings as a white liberal. Nor would I deny that for some reason I was also driven by a desire to be hip and to be cool.

These drives manifested themselves in all facets of the teaching experience. For instance, I was never an authoritarian in any of my contacts with the kids. To the contrary, I am sure that many of the kids would call me a softie or an easy mark. I tended to be lenient with all the rules in the school, mostly because I thought that the rules had no purpose, because I thought them unfair, and because the administration and other teachers were arbitrary in their enforcement of them, but also because I disliked being cast in the role of policeman. Even at things like basketball games, at which I was supposed to guard the doors, I found it hard to turn down the appeal of a person who would "gripe to me" about not having enough money to pay for a ticket to get in. Everything I did seemed to be reminiscent of that first day when I ran up against the boys in the hall who were singing.

Yet it was more than just a matter of being soft because I wanted to be loved. I'm not denying that I often played things for a laugh or dropped an assignment because of a holiday, but there was more to it than that. As I stated earlier, I went into education with the idea of changing things. Very simply, my philosophy of education differed from that of those who were in control.

I didn't like the prescribed course of study. I discarded a curriculum guide that was supposed to be the Bible because I felt it was irrelevant and I taught "controversial subjects" even

though it was against the rules of the Board of Education. I
didn't give out cuts and tardies even though it was required, and
I didn't enforce the dress rules because I thought them to be
class oriented and basically inane as well. It may sound as if I
were an incompetent teacher, but this is not the case. What I
tried to be was a relevant teacher. What I did was to get to know
the kids on an intimate level. I went to football and basketball
games with them. I chaperoned at the dances they had. I ate in
the lunchroom with them, and I talked after school with them.
I fought the disciplinarians and the archaic and inactive student
government with them, and I lent them books and money (something I was told never to do because I'd never see either again—
Not so! I saw all but a few dollars again). After awhile the
students began to trust me. I won their respect by being straight
with them. I was an "OK cat." I was "cool Canfield," "J.C.,"
and "John." "Mr. Canfield is all right."

I remember one time on the way back from a trip to the state
capital; I was walking toward the back of the chartered bus
when one boy said, "Cool it! Here comes a teacher." Then another person said, "It's OK. Mr. Canfield's not a teacher; he's
one of us." Of course the kid was making a typical play at my
ego, but whatever it was they were doing was stopped. I had
been effective. I had done my job without being an ogre in the
process. I never felt that by this kind of attitude I lost respect—
not real respect. Some of the older teachers in the school were a
little startled and upset when they heard a student in the halls
calling me "John" or "J.C.," but merely being called *Mister*
Canfield isn't a sign of real respect. That is the superficial and
sham form that the other teachers demanded. Real respect, it
seems, is something much deeper and much more valuable.

But why all of this? Very simple. I believe very firmly that
one could successfully teach a series of meaningless dates to a
class without any feeling of rapport with the students, but to really
help a person to grow and expand, to become truly educated, is
to do something much more than this. It is to help the student
begin to understand himself, his potentials, and the relation of
both of these to his surrounding world. Most, yet not all, of the
teachers in the school were irrelevant to the lives of the students
whom they taught. A student would quickly identify the teacher
with his or her subject and block them both out of his mind. In

this context part of my message was "Look, baby. I'm not your typical honkie; I'm cool! I play a guitar and play poker, shoot pool and shoot craps, make the parties and make the scenes. But, see, I've got books, too. Books are important because they're important to me, and I'm not a jive cat! Ya dig?" Even more important, though, was the atmosphere of honesty that developed. True educational growth cannot take place without honesty. This was where being one of the gang paid off. We could really talk to each other rather than playing the traditional teacher-student game.

There is a problem, however, with getting that involved with the students. One of the drawbacks is to watch the students that you have in your classroom getting "messed over" by the other members of the school's faculty and administration. One constantly witnesses teachers on hall duty and the building's security police collaring kids in the school and taking them to the principal's office for some form of punishment. Too many times one can see kids being the victims of an arbitrary decision based on the mood of the teacher at any particular moment. The oft-repeated statement, "If you think you're going to get away with that kind of talk with me, you're mistaken," always seemed to reveal more about the speaker than about the student.

A large part of the first year was spent in an overwhelming state of helplessness. The feeling that results from not being able to effectively intervene on behalf of the student is dehumanizing and debasing, especially if one has tried to build up among the students the image of being a person who is involved in the fight for justice. And yet as a first year teacher you are helpless to do anything. You have no real power within the structure itself. I remember several such incidents during my first year. One of my best students was a member of an Afro-American dance group. During the rehearsals for the talent show, she was walking from the girls' washroom to the lounge in which the tryouts were to take place. As is the usual custom of dancers, she was wearing a pair of tights and a sweatshirt. As she rounded the corner approaching the lounge, she met the disciplinarian, who literally pounced on her and screamed in an almost indescribable barrage of words that the rules forbid the wearing of such things in the school. After a useless explanation and appeal to reason the girl was told to go directly to the office to await further action.

I happened to be a witness to this encounter because I also had been waiting to speak to the disciplinarian about recovering a lost hall pass. (It seemed that this magnificent lady was in charge of all the formal as well as the informal means of oppression that existed in the school.) Throughout this entire ordeal I was helpless to intercede on the girl's behalf. When I finally approached the disciplinarian to ask about the hall pass, she and one of her cronies began to retreat down the hall. As I said, "Excuse me, but I'd like to—," I was rebuffed with "Do you always interrupt people so rudely?"

"Excuse me," I replied. "I didn't realize that I was interrupting a formal conversation. I just thought that you were walking down the hall together."

"We were walking to get away from you!" At this point I spun about angrily and walked away, muttering under my breath obscenities that I wished I had the courage and the lack of civility to have said to her face.

It is very hard to wink at the injustices that constantly occur in the school, and yet this is what most of one's colleagues have trained themselves to do, using such rationalizations as "These kids are always looking for trouble" and "It's all because of this Black Power stuff that's going around." The fact that the school had become predominantly black in the last three years provided many new stereotyped rationalizations for these injustices. Verification of this fact was the removal of the student court once the school had become more than fifty percent black.

One small blessing about high school is that the students usually don't cry when they are getting "shot through the grease," as they call it. Mostly they are defiant, in an effort to maintain dignity, I guess. However, in the grade schools this is not the case. This kind of maltreatment is so much more glaring and hard to take with the added wailings of the child. I remember while I was still a student, I had been asked to talk about black history with a group of eighth graders at a neighboring elementary school. As I was leaving, a woman came down the hall dragging a wailing and protesting boy behind her. I asked one of the students with whom I had been talking if the woman had been his mother. No, that was his teacher. I inquired if that kind of thing happened often, and I was told that it did. I don't think

I could have survived that kind of thing for a year. I was tempted then, as I still am today, to reach out and grab the woman's arm and say, "Stop! This kid has a right to be treated like a human being, and even if the kid is wrong, what you're doing to him is not going to help."

It would be unfair to blame all of my feelings of frustration on the administration or the rest of the faculty. Much of it resulted from what I felt was my own incompetence in the classroom. In my fourth period class, there were about seven people out of the forty-two whom I never quite felt I had reached. They would invariably come in late, without their assignments, talk and laugh throughout the period, and do poorly on all tests and whatever papers they saw fit to hand in. The majority of these students could be placed in the "gang member" category. They didn't share the dominant values of the school, the teachers, or the majority of the students, and few things that we did outside of some of the initial discussions caught their attention. I had been told again and again by the veteran teachers that if one were getting to fifty percent of his students he should feel himself to be successful. However, this criterion did not work for me. The successful ones seemed easy to accept; it was the failures that constantly upset me.

There was one in particular that really made me ache. His name was Chuck. He was not like the rest of the seven. He was a loner—a very cool cat whom everyone admired. In addition, Chuck was smart—damn smart. However, all of these talents were not being used to achieve academic success by legitimate means. Chuck was a con man, pure and simple. He conned the girls, the coaches, the principals, the other teachers, but most of all me, and probably most tragically, himself. Chuck reminded me of the cat who would grow up to be a numbers man, a bookie, and—who knows?—maybe even a classic example of the black preacher. At the end of the year I gave him a C minus instead of a D or an F, because I felt it was my fault that I hadn't failed him earlier in order to get him to come to class or to hand in his assignments. He had me convinced he was accepted into college and less than C would keep him out. I was weak. I gave him the grade—not because he deserved it, but because he had the potential to do even better, and I couldn't see his not going to college. The whole relationship with Chuck and my failure to get him on the right track earlier remains one of my most poignant memories.

Despite these problems my fourth period class was generally a well-behaved class, easy to get along with and very responsive and alert. On the other hand, my seventh period class, all of whom were bright, was much harder to deal with. They were noisy. They were impossible to keep quiet unless I was trying to conduct a discussion. Then there was little or no noise, except in side conversations. They were a constant enigma. They performed excellently on homework, papers, and tests, but my primary impression of them was constant inattentiveness and noise. I used to try to convince myself that since they were the smartest they had the most to say. But most of the talk was of dating, football, television programs, and other topics of school gossip. I was later told by one of my supervisors that since they were the highest on the ladder of social mobility, they had the most to risk by being wrong and by being placed in an academic confrontation. They therefore subconsciously avoided this by talking all of the time. While this may have added insight into the situation, it did not ease my frustration at not being better able to facilitate what I thought to be a valuable learning environment.

My eighth period class was the trial of my day. It consisted of two seniors who needed an extra social studies credit for graduation, two highly intelligent freshman girls, two very withdrawn freshmen boys, and twenty-two hell-cats who would never be in any danger of earning the name "teacher's pet." The class might have been manageable except for two catalysts named Joe and David. I say this because the few times they were absent, we had what resembled a class. Joe was very small and David was very fat. I believe they were always trying to get attention in order to compensate for their inadequacies. But understanding the nature of the problem did not necessarily guarantee a solution. I tried to give them responsibility by letting them take roll, a tactic which was contrary to school policy on grounds of legality and contrary to class sentiments on what they felt to be the ground of fairness. Worse yet, it proved ineffective. They simply used it as a means of getting more attention by mispronouncing some names, eliminating others, and creating general havoc by trying to ape my role as teacher. It never failed to be amusing, but it was always destructive to classroom order. Both Joe and David would also get up and walk around the class at will; all manner of exhortations had no effect on them. I would have been content if they had walked around all day without disturbing others. But this they could not do; they ended up pulling some girl's hair or stealing some boy's hat. I tried sending them to the principal—but only once, for both times they failed to reach the office. I realized that it was my problem and that I would have to handle it myself. Discussions, punishments, rewards, cajolings, admonishments, public embarrassments, positive reinforcements, and negative reinforcements—none of these worked. The school was not prepared to deal with them except by expulsion, and I was not prepared to assume the responsibility for that. And yet I was not prepared to deal with them either. It got so that I hated eighth period. I looked forward to it with apprehension and self-doubt. In the eyes of the school, I was not failing. None of my kids were in the hall, and there were no "undue disturbances." But I knew I was failing.

I brought in movies, had exercises with the newspaper, had the class write their own newspaper, did map exercises, and had them work on problems I brought in, but I felt that I was only occupying them—a sort of military holding action. I sensed no growth. I felt like Mr. Jonas, the teacher I had observed the year before on the West side. What a disappointing self-image! I began watching the clock, hoping the minutes would race by. They never did. It seemed like an eternity before the bell would ring. It would finally come, and I would drag myself to the first floor and prepare to get away from it all. Thank God it was my last class. I would be completely drained of emotional and psychic energy. Some days I would come home and fall asleep from four o'clock to ten o'clock. I am sure it was a symbolic return to the womb.

The next morning I would be reborn again and I would trudge off to school to face another day of trying to be a teacher. Discipline and control are problems that all teachers face. The social studies teacher faces others specific to his academic domain. He is cast as the political science expert on the immediate situation, and he must be able to come up with some viable answers when the students ask, "What are we going to do about this rotten mess we are in?" It was these kinds of questions that reinforced my belief that teaching was going to be tougher than just knowing all the facts gathered together in my graduate history courses. The standard answers about the procedures of the traditional political system are insufficient, but I feel that the same is true of the answer of violent revolutionary change which is so current among the students of the inner city.

If my students were to understand the implications of violence versus nonviolence—the topic they had chosen to study in a preference poll—they were going to have to go where the action was and see the arguments being hashed out where it really counted. Had I not been involved in some social change myself, I probably would not have been able to provide some of the answers that teachers are supposed to have in order to act as the guides that teachers are supposed to be. There were, indeed, some groups dedicated to social change, which could provide direct experience for my students.

The first Saturday that I took a group of students to participate in meetings of such a group was one of the most moving experiences of my life. Jesse Jackson, Sidney Poitier, Dick Gregory, Robert Culp, Oscar Brown Jr., and the leader of a local street gang were all there. Here were people deep in the heart of the racial conflict that was dividing our nation. Here were people trying to resolve the very issues that my classes were struggling with. Here in one room was where it was at. Somehow it was my job as teacher to convey this to my students. This was what life was all about at the moment, and what was the job of teacher but to help his students discover what life was all about?

One of the problems with being this kind of teacher is that every week something new emerges as "the thing that the student needs to know" more than anything else. What this means, then, is that curriculum must be a flexible and constantly changing thing if it is to be relevant and meaningful to the student. The danger with this, though, is the possibility of the lack of any structure. What must be provided all along, and illustrated by events as they happen, is a larger superstructure drawn from a study of historical and sociological data. It is here that the teacher must be a careful analyst of what is happening and be able to help the student place the experiences of his world into an overall framework that is being constantly built throughout the year. This is not a very easy task. In my first attempt at it I am sure that I confused many of my students more than I helped them. However, I still feel that this is the goal that should be sought.

Students were not the only people that I confused during the course of the year. When one is a new teacher, he is looked upon as some kind of threatening animal which is ready to prey upon the older teachers, to turn the students against them, and to subvert the social order that they have carefully constructed over the many years that they have been there. Any innovation that one tries in the classroom or in operation of the school is looked upon as incompetence, negligence, malfeasance, or what is even worse, treason.

If one wished to take his students on a field trip, he was cross-examined at various levels as to the nature and purpose of the trip and was usually discouraged from its undertaking with stories of control problems, transportation difficulties and substitution difficulties. If one wished to eliminate a portion of the curriculum for something he felt was more relevant to the particular needs of the students at that time, he was reprimanded for not performing his task properly, or was questioned (even by members of other departments) as to what he was doing.

I remember once when I showed an award-winning movie on the concentration camps in Germany during World War II to illustrate a point about man's inhumanity to man during times of war, my students reacted to the movie with what I felt was the proper amount of repulsion and shock. The older teachers, on the other hand, were up in arms about the showing of this film and made it a point of one of our very infrequent teachers' meetings. With the exception of the few Jewish teachers on the faculty, who supported my showing of the film, the other teachers either supported the attack or stood by in quiet acquiescence.

This kind of censure became most intense when six teachers—two who were black and four who were white—sponsored an Afro-American club at the school. Since ninety-seven percent of the student body was black, and since there was very little attention paid to black history, literature, and culture in the classroom, we felt, with several of the students, that such a club was very badly needed. The response of the majority students was very enthusiastic. The initial response of the teachers was only apathy. It was only later, after a disturbance following the commemora-

tion of the death of Malcolm X, that the faculty began to use the
club as a scapegoat for all the problems in the school. The majority of the faculty could not come to grips with the fact that the
students, along with the rest of the nation, were in a new state of
ferment. Rather than admit this, they began to blame all the
difficulties they encountered on the club. Several of the sponsors
began to receive African coins in their mailboxes. We interpreted
this as a reminder that if they did not like it in the United States
they were welcome to return to Africa. In addition to other forms
of harassment, unsigned letters, cartoons, and editorials from
newspapers were constantly found in our mailboxes. Below is
one such item, of which we received Xeroxed copies. To my
chagrin I have never been able to determine the source of this
racist poem:

The Negro's Twenty-third Psalm

LBJ is my shepherd;
I shall not work.
He maketh me to lie down in front of theatres;
He restoreth my welfare check.
He leadeth me in the path of sit-ins for Communism's sake.
Yea, though I walk through the Heart of Dixie,
I shall fear no police, for L.B.J. is with me;
His tear gas and federal troops comfort me.
He prepareth a table for me in the presence of white folks;
He anointeth my head with anti-kink straightener.
My Cadillac trunk spilleth over;
Surely the Supreme Court will follow me all the days of my life
And I shall dwell in a federal housing project forever.

Yea-man.

This kind of racism, I think, is one more reason why I identified
with the kids more than with the other teachers in the school.

Later in the year we received unsigned copies of a letter that
one of the teachers had sent to the editor of a local newspaper. In
the letter the author stated flatly that there were communists in
the school who were trying to cause dissatisfaction and revolt
among the students and disorder and chaos among the faculty.
The author also stated that she had called the FBI, the sheriff's
office, the state police, and the office of the district superin-

tendent of schools without any effect. Now that she had written this letter, she hoped, something would be done about this terrible menace to society. The incidents that precipitated these letters also caused divisions among the faculty that were not healed even by the end of the year. One attempt by the Board of Education to smooth things out—the devotion of an entire school day to a human relations seminar staffed by board personnel—failed to alleviate the situation significantly. It did, however, manage to start a few people talking about the problems in a more rational manner.

One important part of the educational process that is not as readily apparent as the teachers and the students during the first year is that represented by the parents. The experiences that I had with parents were very mixed, but all were emotionally upsetting. When one is dealing with a student, either in or out of the classroom, that student may appear as an individual entity with his own hang-ups, goals, and aspirations. But the situation is seldom as simple as that, for the student also represents the goals and aspirations of his parents. This may be a good or a bad thing, depending on how the goals and aspirations of the student mesh with those of the parents.

The parents of children in black schools, more than other parents, seem to place a greater hope in education as the panacea for all the problems of their children and their society. From one year's experience I would argue that this hope is an unfounded one; nevertheless, the belief still prevails that a good education (usually interpreted as good grades) will solve all the problems. It is very easy to forget how concerned these parents are about this matter; however, there are times when it is brought home very painfully. One such incident occurred after several social studies teachers had taken a group of students to the state capital at Springfield. The trip had cost each of the students eleven dollars. This paid for the busses, the guided tour, and the food, and it left about three dollars to help defray the cost of books for the history department that were not provided for in the budget.

During the beginning of the year, I had thought that eleven dollars would have been too great a strain on the budgets of most of the kids. But after I had seen all of the souvenir buying that went on during that trip, I didn't feel so bad about the eleven dollar cost. However, as we arrived home that night, about eleven o'clock, one bus was late. As we were explaining to the waiting parents why the other bus had been delayed, one of them began to talk about the trip. "I hope these kids learned something today," he said. "I hope the sacrifices that we parents make have some effect on what these kids learn. Eleven dollars is a lot of money. I hope they learned something as a result of this trip." I wasn't really at all sure that they had learned something; in fact, I was sure that there were several who hadn't. I began to feel very bad at that moment. Suddenly all of the fun had been taken out of the trip. But here I was reassuring the man that they had learned quite a bit about the history of the state and about the important things that take place in the state government. For several days I was very depressed by this whole incident.

Unfortunately, not all parents are as concerned about the education of their children as the man was that night. On the contrary, many are so unconcerned that they make the education of their children virtually impossible. I remember one girl in my homeroom who was very brilliant according to the battery of tests that the students submit to during their twelve years of education. However, she had what teachers commonly refer to as "a home problem." Her parents were less than cordial to her and to each other. This was caused by a drinking father and a promiscuous mother. The child, who was a freshman, was just beginning to discover the great potential that she herself had for getting into trouble, and she was beginning to emulate the behavior of her mother in very specific terms. As her school attendance record became a problem, the parents were called in for the customary parent conference with the personnel of the attendance office. The parents did not appear at the designated time. After a second appointment was made and not kept, the child was declared truant. The parents were contacted by a truant officer who informed them of their legal responsibility. Then a new conference was scheduled—this time with the parents and the child's counselor. At this meeting it became quite apparent that the parents looked upon the child as a mere liability, something which was in the way rather than something to be loved and cared for.

The parents of the child offered her no guidance or direction. The mother wanted no part of the girl. The father was a little different. In his more sober moments he felt a great deal of guilt about his neglect of the child, and he promised to take her to live with him. This never materialized. Meanwhile, the girl was getting deeper into trouble. Her circle of friends was becoming worse all the time, her grades were terrible, and her attendance was falling off even more. The father was finally induced to enroll her in a private school where she would get more individualized attention and where her activities would be more carefully supervised.

Even after all of this, one cannot help but feel sorry for the girl and somehow resent the parents for their lack of care for the child. Although one can intellectually understand the forces in our society that cause these situations, it is very difficult for one to face objectively the consequences of them. One very easily falls into blaming the nearest things, such as the parents, the counselors, the teachers, and the police rather than the real forces that cause these situations to arise in the first place.

Parents are a lot like students. They fall into no one specific category other than that they all have children who are attending your school. They have varying levels of intelligence, education, articulateness, social awareness, sensitivity, income, manners, and compassion. This was at no time more clearly shown during the year than when several people attempted to form a group of concerned parents to work on the problems of the schools and the police that affected their children. Several of the teachers who had earlier voiced their dissatisfaction with the schools were also invited. The aim of the first meeting was to help delineate the exact problems that existed so that the parents' group could begin to work on them. The meeting was an amazing social revelation. The diversity of the people who had come to the meeting was manifest in the clothes that were worn. There was everything from business suits and the uniforms of bus drivers to work clothes and African dress. The attitudes and opinions that these people held were equally diverse.

At the beginning of the meeting one of the organizing parents introduced two of the students who had been beaten by the police in the latest disturbance that had taken place at the school after the death of Dr. Martin Luther King, Jr. During a memorial service that was being held in the auditorium for the juniors and seniors, the freshmen and sophomores were waiting in their regular homerooms, supposedly under the supervision of their homeroom teachers. However, due to the great amount of confusion resulting from the changed schedule and from the nature of the event, many of the students were wandering through the halls. One of these students pulled a fire alarm. The students in the assembly were told to stay in their seats while the freshmen and sophomores went outside. Many of the teachers, fearing violence, stayed in the school, leaving those students who went outside for the most part unsupervised. Police were called because there was a student "mob" outside the school building. When the police arrived they acted irrationally, in the opinion of many of the students and teachers, in their efforts to restore order to the school. At this juncture one of the policemen was shoved. Whether this was accidental or on purpose has never been established. The policeman lashed out in an uncontrolled fit of anger and began to strike the people nearest to him, seriously injuring one male student and unnecessarily beating several other girls who happened to be near. There were several witnesses who confirmed this, and consequently the student who was charged with the offense was exonerated in subsequent court action.

School had been let out, and for the remainder of the day students were harassed all over the area neighboring the school. One student was picked up while standing across the street from his own house. He was formally charged with "disorderly conduct," but the kids referred to all the arrests that occurred this day as having been made for "not moving fast enough" or for "being at the right place at the wrong time."

At any rate, two of the students who were involved in these arrests were telling the assembled parents about what was happening to them when a dispute broke out over the purpose of the meeting. The organizing parents explained that this first meeting was one of information in order to help the parents better understand what the problems of the community were, so that what had happened to these children would not have to happen to theirs. Many of what appeared to be the more affluent parents said that they were sure that the students who had been arrested probably deserved it in the first place and that this could not possibly happen to their children. Their children had been brought up properly!

This naturally offended the parents of those who had been arrested. At this point an executive board of the PTA (all women) got into the act by protesting the need for action by this ad hoc group, arguing that the PTA was the proper channel for all such activity. The organizing parents argued that many of the people, both husbands and wives, had to work during the days to pay off mortgages on their homes and to send their children to college. Since the PTA met during the day, it was impossible for them to come to meetings. Then one of the parents attacked a man who had defended the PTA, saying that it was nice if one were a lawyer like the previous speaker, but that those who worked for a living could not possibly attend. As what seemed to be a class conflict began to surface, one of the mothers who would fall into the more affluent group asked me if this was a "Black Power" meeting. I asked her what she meant by that, and she was a little miffed that I might possibly be in sympathy with anyone who advocated Black Power. However, I assured her that the meeting was not called by any Black Power organization that I knew of. This did not appease her at all. Many of the people in the front of the room were using words such as "Black" and "Afro-American." At this point the woman got together with some of her social friends and walked out of the meeting. Thereafter the meeting began to disintegrate into personality conflicts, while the issues were all but forgotten. The last several speakers might have saved the meeting had they come first, but the people who really needed to hear the message had left by then. The meeting ended with a lot of confusion, hostility, disparity, and despair. This was to be the character of all such meetings with parents for the rest of the year.

In trying to work with parents on issues that concern their schools, I found a very definite deference to the established authority of the school and its administration. This deference is the result of a combination of many forces. For the successful, school represents the path of success that they followed. They are willing to accept many of the injustices and inequities that the school contains in exchange for its sociological use as a ticket to $ucce$$. They equate respect for authority (be it just or unjust) with the achievement of a very necessary self-control. What they fail to stop and ask themselves is just what is a good education and what is not.

The entire day of our school's open house I met only the parents of one student. As could be expected, they were the parents of one of my "A" students. How disappointing! Yet this can be explained. Many of the parents who did not come were them-

selves the victims of bad schools either in the North or the South.
Many of them never graduated from high school. They were
dropouts of a generation ago and now they find themselves in the
peculiar situation of having their own children in school. They
are as afraid of school now as they were fifteen years ago. In
addition, the black community and other similarly disenfranchised
communities have always had a history of defeat when attempting
reform. Many of these people have been defeated so·many times
and on so many different fronts that they are just tired of trying.
They have never had success, and they see nothing to make them
believe that they shall have it now. There is a "what's-the-use"
attitude that prevails in many of these communities.

As bleak as this situation may seem at first glance, a radical
change is nevertheless taking place. There is a growing awareness
in the black community that things aren't "the way it's s'posed
to be." This awareness of the realities of racist America, both in
her present social structure and in her past history, has led to a
redefinition of the way things are and were, and to a growing
unity manifest in Black consciousness, Black pride, and Black
Power. There are some parents in the black community who are,
and who are becoming, politically aware. They are the indigenous
leaders, the community organizers, the teachers, the social
workers, the organization lawyers, and more and more, the man
on the street. Whether they be Negroes, Afro-Americans, Mus-
lims, or black men, they are being educated by their children and
by their neighbors, they are getting themselves together into
organizations; and most importantly, they are beginning to openly
fight for what is rightfully theirs.

This same type of split exists among the students, but I found
the proportion of people in each category to be reversed. At the
beginning of the year the students in my school could be divided
into three major groups: "the clique," the regular guys, and the
"gang-bangers." The traditional group of athletes was to be found
in the first two.

The clique would correspond to the usual social elite group
found in any school. These were typically the college bound,
those who sported Brooks Brothers shirts and *Seventeen* fashions,
the members of the clubs and sororities, and the powers in the
student government. They played in the band, sang in the glee
club, ran the student newspaper, and were generally the teachers'

pets. To me they were the snobs, the machines, the cop-outs, the
"Toms," the uncreative thinkers, the rote learners, and generally
nothing more than representatives of a repugnant status quo.

The regular guys were the students who weren't in the clique
but who weren't in the gangs either. They played football and
baseball, made C's and B minuses, worked after school, belonged
to no clubs, were not usually in trouble, showed the proper
amount of respect for everybody, and generally finished school
and got a hard-working job. They were everybody's solid citizens
—loyal, apathetic, and unambitious. While few of these kids were
outstanding, almost all were very likeable, for they were very real
people. Only their apathy was disturbing.

The gang-bangers, or more simply "bangers," were those who
belonged to the local youth gangs in the neighborhood. These
were the kids who were the hard core truants, who shot craps,
who drank wine, who smoked pot, who got into fights at the
football games, who constantly became the drop-outs and
"force-outs," whose girls were always pregnant, and whose parents were always absent. And yet this same group had the re-
deeming factor of seeing more clearly than anyone else what an
absurd and irrelevant institution their school system was.

With the exception of the few remaining white kids, this com-
prised the social situation. By January there were only about
forty white students left, and they broke down into two basic
groups: the liberals and the bigots. The latter group constantly
segregated themselves from the rest of the student body, in addition to being the first ones to question anything that the black
students did. In all of my classes I had only three white students,
all of whom were very tolerant and understanding. Nevertheless,
I had casual contact with most of the others. I remember that
some of the white students were very cruel to each other. I remember one incident when a white girl who had defended Black
Power was given a bottle of tanning lotion by the rest of the white
boys. The leader of this group had once told me that he and his
family were going to move to Australia because there were virtually no Negroes there.

As the year progressed, a significant change began to take
place in the social structure. This was the growth of Black consciousness and of the belief in Black Power. There are several
reasons for this. The preceding summer of 1967 had been marked

by eight major riots in urban areas across the country. During August a Black Power conference had been held in Newark, New Jersey. In that same week Congress had defeated President Johnson's rat-control bill. Earlier in the summer Chicago had witnessed the formation of Operation Breadbasket. The aim of the organization was to keep black-earned dollars in the black community by supporting the purchasing of black products, the founding of black-owned businesses, banking in black banks, and creating jobs for black people in the stores and businesses that are located in the black community. Muhammad Ali had been stripped of his boxing crown and taken to court for his refusal to fight in what he felt was an unjust war in Vietnam. Late in August Stokely Carmichael and Charles Hamilton published their book *Black Power*. On an international scene civil war had broken out in Nigeria and the problems of apartheid were becoming more glaring and were causing strife in the Union of South Africa. The winds of change could hardly be missed. Everyone everywhere was talking of Black Power. Our high school was no exception.

Several girls in the school decided that they wanted to start a club to study their Afro-American heritage and culture, to redefine themselves and the society in which they lived, and to begin to work toward some positive goals within a black framework. The response was overwhelming. There were several hundred students at the first few meetings, and all were very eager to pursue the goals which they outlined. Over the course of the year formal attendance dropped off, but active interest continued to grow and to manifest itself in many ways. Those who belonged to the clique never showed much interest in the club for it threatened the middle-class values upon which their social system was built. The other two groups in school showed great enthusiasm for the club and for the pursuit of a black identity.

The change that took place among many of the students was remarkable. For the first time students who had never read a complete book before would be seen carrying copies of works such as *The Autobiography of Malcolm X, Malcolm X Speaks, Manchild in the Promised Land, Message to the Blackman,* and *Before the Mayflower*. Both boys and girls began to wear natural hair styles and African dress. Some of the students began to study African languages at Saturday morning classes. City-wide student organizations were formed, and there were exchanges with other clubs and black high schools. There was a new electrifying spark of pride, curiosity, and intellectual challenge surging throughout the students of the school.

John Munro, past dean of Harvard College and presently teaching in Birmingham, Alabama, stated in an article in *Time* magazine that if black students first gained a positive identity through the study of black history and literature, everything else, such as biology and calculus, would come naturally and easily. This thesis also proved true in our school. Students who were contemplating dropping out of school stayed and earned As in some courses. Others who were perennial D and F students began to show marked improvement in their work. Many past troublemakers now searched for positive reform within the school. It was both amazing and gratifying to watch the metamorphosis in some of the students.

It was things such as this—the metamorphosis of a student—that made teaching worthwhile. This was as true inside the classroom as it was outside of it. With all the pressures and failures that I met with throughout the year in my attempts to bring structural change to the school, I think I should have died in a state of depression had there not been some success in the classroom. Gratification came in many forms. Every once in a while a student who had been quiet all year would open up and voice a brilliant insight—to the astonishment of everyone present, often including himself. Occasionally a class discussion would take a sharp turn in a surprising direction that I could never have predicted, or the level of the discussion would be carried higher than I ever dreamed possible. Sometimes a unit would strike a student in such a way that he would get all A's and afterward would say something like, "You know, I really liked that unit on law. I think I'll become a lawyer." Sometimes it would be one individual who would amaze me, such as the time Johnny, who would never read anything or turn in an assignment, borrowed a copy of *Nigger* by Dick Gregory. He finished the book in one night and handed in a report on it two days later. Then again it might be an entire class that finally pulls together on a project that you were never really sure they could do. I remember specifically the time at the end of the year when I decided to let my freshman class do some independent study on Afro-American history. I brought in about forty paperback books with varied reading levels and areas of interest and let the class choose which they wanted to read. After they chose their books, I was stunned by the silence as they sat engrossed in their books. Was this the same class that usually drove me up a wall every day? What a revelation!

These same feelings of satisfaction and joy would also come while grading papers. Occasionally a paper would reflect a bold leap or analysis or interpretation that would take me by surprise and lift my otherwise depressed spirits. I remember also that if, while grading I would go down the answer blanks and see no mistakes, I would glance at the name at the top of the page and would begin rooting for this kid at each question as I continued grading the test. Then to see the smile on the student's face as I handed back an A would really lift me up. But as I stated earlier, for each victory there is a concomitant trial. For every A handed back, there is an F or an unexpected D or C. Nothing is more disheartening than to see tears well up in the eyes of a child as he receives his unsuccessful paper, or to hear a student tell you that, while you were giving him a B for working so hard, he failed English and math.

I also had some very definite feelings of success when I helped to coach the varsity swimming team. I found coaching to be very different from teaching. The relationships that were established with the kids were much deeper, and the rewards were more immediate. Success could be measured in precise times and visible skills. The skills that one attempts to build in a classroom are much more subtle and hard to measure. It is hard to discern the degree of attitude change, but it is easy to see a person finally get his head turning correctly when he swims.

Since this was the first time in three years that the school had had a swimming team, we didn't win any meets, but we did have many individuals win in their own events. We also were able to build up a great deal of team spirit and pride over the course of the season. This is another thing that is next to impossible to achieve in class. The rewards of classwork are too far in the future for anyone to get excited about them the same way that he can get turned on by beating a rival school.

As I look back over the year, the victories—large and small— seem to stand out above the failures. There were many successes to take some measure of credit for. Only one of my students failed, and that was for excessive absences. Several others graduated and will be going to college, while yet others graduated into good jobs and will be very competent nurses, printers, and shop mechanics. But not all of the successes were academic. Many kids found themselves and their identities over the course of the year, and many of these began to organize to do something about it. And somehow I don't think I'll ever forget the class officer who refused to submit his graduation speech to the senior sponsor for approval. When the time for his speech came during the graduation, he arose, explained the situation, and finished with, "If that's the way they want to be, to hell with speeches!" While I'm sure that it was he himself who was entirely responsible for his action, I took a little bit of credit for that one, too. He had acted like a man in his reaction against censorship, and I was proud of him.

The end of the year came suddenly. One morning I woke up and I didn't go to school anymore. That was it. Somehow even with kids running around school to get their yearbooks autographed, with graduation rehearsals taking place, and with final grades being given out, the end just seemed to come without any warning or preparation.

And so many things were just really starting. As an aftermath of the election of a student government for the forthcoming year, many groups formed in protest against the clique's getting all the offices and against the really powerless structure upon which the entire process of elections and the student government were based. The Afro-American Club was beginning to change its focus in the direction of more effectively dealing with the affairs of its members in relation to the school. But best of all was the fact that many of the teachers, as a result of the human-relations day held at the school, were beginning to band together into enlightened groups to push for change.

I didn't want the year to end, and I didn't want to leave that school. Unfortunately, all but one of our progressive group were not returning. For several different administrative reasons, we were unable to return to the school even though we all wanted to very badly. It's like all of our "friends" are going to get messed over by the administration and other "Toms, biddies, and bitches," as one girl put it. Secondly, it's just leaving an unfinished job. One member of the graduating class summed it up nicely when he wrote the following in my yearbook:

To John, I was never in any of your classes (lucky for you)
but I learned from you an important lesson—look at an issue
from both sides and be more objective, and due to you, Johnson, and Wilson, I got interested in the Afro-American Club.
But one thing, why don't you ever win around here? You didn't
get the literary magazine because the establishment took it, you
still remain the antagonist, and the swim team winless. I'll miss
getting on your case, too. Good luck.

Already I miss those kids. I loved them as people, as individuals, and as friends. It is impossible to work intensively for a
whole year with somebody and not either love or hate them. I miss
talking to them and teasing them. It is a great experience watching people grow for such a long time, and it is very difficult to be
suddenly cut off from these same people. I must sound like a
mother just separated from her children, but the feelings I have
are that deep. I understand all too well why the students cried at
graduation. There is a great feeling of loss. I'm sure that this is a
very selfish feeling, but it exists nevertheless. It probably wouldn't
be so hard if I knew that I were returning, for there would always
be enough students who were also returning to provide a sense
of continuity rather than the total separation that I felt.

Right now I am working at a Women's Job Corps Center as a
curriculum writer. The girls here are very similar to the students
that I left behind in Chicago, but not being in the classroom is
very disturbing to me. Contact with the students is much more
strained and difficult. I wish that I were once again teaching.
Teaching is like a bug, and now that I've caught it I can't seem
to shake it. I'm sure that as the year goes on I shall come to know
the corpswomen more closely, but what I really look forward to
is returning to the inner city in Chicago and once again doing
my thing.

There is only one thing that could prevent that—the Black
Power movement which wants black schools run and staffed by
black people. That very handily excludes me. Throughout the
year I had arguments with the other coach of the swimming team
about the role of the white man in the black schools. It was a
very schizophrenic relationship. While he liked me as a friend,
his black militancy hated me for being white. I found that several kids had the same hangup with my being white. I am no

John Brown, because I believe in nonviolence; but I do believe very strongly in Black Power, and I fully understand why the militants have often resorted to force and violence to bring about change. I am not "whitey" and I am no "Tom." I am sure that I still have undiscovered prejudices, but not nearly so many as some of the middle-class Negro teachers in the school. I feel that I very successfully related to the students I taught this past year, and I feel that I played a beneficial role in their education.

All I want to do is teach the kids that I dig. The philosophy of Black Power and black nationalism, however, says that I should go to the suburbs and teach white kids not to be bigots. I question my ability to do that. I feel that a teacher should live in the neighborhood where he teaches and not be an outsider. I couldn't live in suburbia and be comfortable. I would feel trapped. I really feel much freer in the black community because here is where the life-blood of America is presently coming from. Here is where the most valid criticism of America is being articulated; here is where people are beautiful, and freedom is a meaningful term. Here is where I want to be—teaching.

Gail Richardson

X Is for the Unknown

I was going to be a good teacher—interesting and fair and encountering my students as people. I would regard each of the students as an individual having dignity and worth. I would create a class atmosphere that was friendly and encouraging, in which a person could make a mistake without being made to feel that he was an idiot. I was not going to teach mathematics; I was going to teach students mathematics. I would communicate my enthusiasm for the subject; not all students would share it, necessarily, but they would at least see it.

These imprecise, flattering notions of myself as teacher were the thoughts that brought me to Belden High School. I knew little of the school, other than that it was large (over three thousand students) and in a "changing" neighborhood. The once predominantly white upper-middle-class student body was now heterogeneous with respect to both race and income level, serving blacks, whites, Puerto Ricans, and Mexicans from middle and lower class backgrounds. Because of crowded conditions, the school ran an eleven-period day, where each student attended eight consecutive periods: typically, five classes, lunch, and two study halls.

Despite my optimistic self-concept, my expectations for the year did not reflect complete confidence, for I was uncertain of at least three areas: grading, discipline, and parental contacts were fearsome unknowns. I did feel that these issues would cease to be problems as I gained experience.

60

In addition to these role expectations, I also held preconceived notions about classroom mechanics. I anticipated three classes of no more than thirty-five students each. I hoped to receive copies of my text before school began, so that I could begin planning. I was worried about what I would do on the first day.

From that first day, all of my optimistic visions were gradually but steadily eclipsed by the reality which confronted me.

Actually, there were two first days. On Tuesday we arrived at the school to find teachers milling about the office. I located my mailbox, which contained unfamiliar materials of assorted sizes and descriptions and a copy of the day's agenda. One of the office personnel directed me to a box of large manila envelopes, and I found one with my name on it. Inside was a list of students in my homeroom.

In the morning all of the teachers were addressed by the school administration. The lady in charge of programming explained that data processing had gone berserk with some of the class rosters; this information left all of the math teachers wondering which of them had the class of forty-nine students. She also explained that all classes would be leveled as soon as possible, and that everyone should be patient and keep every student assigned to him until officially moved from class, "even if they have to sit on the windowsills." I laughed with the others at what I was sure was an exaggeration.

The homeroom teachers then went to the lunchroom, where they located the cards belonging to students in their homerooms. My first task as a teacher was to separate thirty-two sets of program cards along perforations and to sort them into six piles. My homeroom was now a list of names and a pack of program cards, and I had had a taste of homeroom work—time-consuming, clerical, and done by teachers because there was no one else to do it.

Departmental meetings were held after lunch, and there I met the nine other math teachers. At that time we received our class rosters; my class sizes were seven, thirty-five, and thirty-five. Some useful information concerning supplies was given. Then came the shock: it was not clear when we would receive books, or even which ones would be used.

I arrived home tired and discouraged. The other teachers had seemed nice enough, but there had been no time to talk to any of them during the programmed portion of the day. I was sure the returning teachers knew what would happen the next day when the students arrived, but I also realized that I did not even know what questions to ask. Only by borrowing a copy of the "Opening Day Instructions" did I know how long the periods would be. I found that situation particularly irritating. The copies had been prepared at the end of the previous school year. Thus all of the returning teachers had them, but there was an insufficient number for the people who needed help most of all.

From instructions given in the morning meeting I knew that I was to distribute one set of program cards, assign lockers, distribute and re-collect status cards, and take roll; this was to be done in a forty-minute homeroom period which opened the day. Luckily the students in my homeroom were new to the school, and I had three guide sheets to give to each. By reading these ahead of the students, I was able to get some idea of hall regulations, lunchroom regulations, and attendance procedures.

The students in my classes were as yet only lists of names, many of which were unpronounceable, and one of my classrooms had little board space. Whatever hopes I had of doing bulletin boards vanished when I realized I was teaching in an art room and two science rooms—clearly, one period in a room used for as many as eleven classes does not rate bulletin board space. My textbooks would arrive possibly by Monday, and I would not see them until the students did. All the insecure feelings which had accompanied me into the school were intensified by the day's events. Ignorance seemed synonymous with incompetence. How could I possibly have thought I was going to be good?

The only thing over which I had control was the twenty-minute class period. I decided to begin with some ground rules. I wanted to make as few as possible, and finally came up with three rules dealing with courtesy and respect for others, and with homework.

I also planned presentations dealing with the mathematical topic, set theory, for both the algebra and essential mathematics classes.

I then went to bed, fervently wishing that school began on the second or third day and not on the first.

The second "first" day was a great relief. The students were cooperative, their names not nearly as unpronounceable as imagined, the system a little less incomprehensible. Homeroom was a rush, but I accomplished everything. An uncertain moment had occurred when one of the group asked if he should turn in his course book. What in heaven's name was a course book? A show of hands indicating clear majority, I called for them. What I was supposed to do with them then was anybody's guess.

The twenty-minute classes went well. I was so nervous during the first class that I destroyed a paper clip by bending and twisting it as I talked, and I paced the front of the room constantly. Twenty-one students reported to that class—no surprise, since I did not really believe that I would have only seven. The other classes were of the predicted size. The students were very quiet and attentive, and I managed to get some responses to my questions. I told them that they could sit where they pleased until Friday, when a seating chart would be made from their positions on that day.

It was surprising to me that merely knowing what my classes looked like could be such a relief. The fact that I would not have texts until Monday was not upsetting any longer, because my "audience" was now known. The first day's reception was encouraging and gave me more confidence about the remainder of the week. But the most important effect of those first-day classes was that tomorrow's classes would be filled with familiar faces.

I am fairly certain that had I been educated in the Chicago schools, much of the first-day routines would have been familiar to me: clearly, I would have at least known what a course book was. But I was totally new to the system, and I was terribly ignorant of procedures and most concerned about doing the right thing. And because I felt I had no sources to help me know about these things, those first few days were needlessly nerve-racking.

The First Month

New students continued to report to class, and by the third week I was running out of desks. My class sizes were now forty-one, forty-one, and thirty-nine, and in the science rooms several students were sitting on folding chairs in the aisles. The principal effect of the increased class sizes was that I no longer felt that I was keeping everyone's interest, or that it was possible to do so.

The quiet atmosphere had dissipated by this time; my students decided that I was no tyrant and hoped that I might be a push-over. This was especially true of the two afternoon classes. I was too tolerant of their constant talking. Sarcasm was lost on them, and I avoided the direct approach for the first month; I felt un-comfortable telling people to "stop talking." The need for such a reminder was not consistent with the interest I was supposed to be generating, and to utter it was an admission of failure. My patience was remarkable, but ridiculous in retrospect.

At first, teaching was very much like acting. I wrote down nearly everything I planned to say, all of the examples I intended to use, and every question I wanted to ask. This kept me near the desk, close to the script; and if I got too far away, it forced me to return to find my place. I frequently heard myself as though someone else were talking, as though I were playing a role, the role of "Interesting Teacher."

By the fourth week, the feeling of being on stage was begin-ning to fade. I was still planning, but in less detail. The main points were listed, special examples recorded, and leading ques-tions jotted down. I still had to refer to my program, but was able to stay away from it for longer periods of time. I did not worry about unexpected questions, partly because I seldom had any, and also because I had successfully handled the few that had arisen. I began to sound like myself to my own listening ear, and I felt more comfortable.

Guard duty was most distasteful. Every teacher in the school taught five periods each day, ate lunch during one period, and had one period free for preparation. In addition, nearly every teacher also had one period of supervision—a hall-guard post or a study hall. That was what I called "guard duty." Mine was study hall, which met in one large room containing about two hundred desks. I knew only five of the students; the rest did not know whether I was a teacher or a student teacher. The two other teachers—who had been assigned to the study hall before I was—stayed near the front, and I walked around and asked, or told, the back section to be quiet. The trick seemed to lie in acting casual enough about the situation so that the students did not feel they were putting something over on me by talking when my back was turned.

Complications were introduced in the person of a student as-sistant who was allowed by one of the other teachers to visit with other students. One day I had sole charge of this section, and things nearly got out of hand when I asked the boy to be quiet. He had been talking to five students, and nearly everyone else in the room was quiet. I walked over, knowing I was asking for trouble. I asked him, by name, to stop talking, and then wandered away. Some subtle owl noises were directed toward my back. I made a complete circuit of the room; the talking continued. I then moved one student whom I discovered sitting in the wrong place. I said no more, but walked around again. Back at the desk, I checked several names on the seating chart and found boys sitting in girls' places and vice versa. The talkers had switched themselves around, and since the assistant knew everybody, he had had no difficulty in taking roll. My first impulse was anger, because they had beaten me. Then I realized that the period was nearly over, that there would be nothing gained in being angry, and that this was part of the game. I never mentioned the incident to the other teachers.

I remembered a scene I had witnessed a few days earlier, when our study hall was told to meet in the cafeteria because our regular room was being used for testing. The result had been great confusion since another study hall was already in session in the auditorium. One of our boys had done something which greatly angered one of the male teachers who ran the cafeteria study hall. He chewed the boy out, which caused other students to hoot; then he turned to the group and shouted, "I want this place quiet," hitting chairs with a ruler as he walked back to the front. Rather than intimidating them, this action only made the students more scornful. I thought the whole business exaggerated and decided that, while there was a place for legitimate anger, such histrionics were ineffectual, if not degrading.

On another occasion, when our study hall was again moved to the cafeteria, the same teacher made his announcement about a quiet study, then came over to me and said that if any of the boys gave me any trouble, I should signal to him and he would take care of it. I thanked him, but was irritated by his attitude. I thought to myself (and thought that I should have told him, but did not), "I am not anticipating any trouble." Because I was not. My study hall was not a group of convicts anxious to make their escape by throwing me over the balcony. "Guilty until proven innocent" seemed to be the guiding principle, and this teacher was not the only one who subscribed to it. I was determined that I would never treat students as rudely as did some of the teachers. I suspected that some of the students were real troublemakers, but it was terrible to assume the worst of them all.

Another incident which upset me occurred in that first month. After two weeks, one of the students in my homeroom finally turned up. What the counselor told me about this student made me want to cry: the student had been at school on the first day, but he did not know where his homeroom was meeting. Someone told him to go to the office and look at my program. He went to the office but did not know where to look (it took *me* two days to realize what those cards were). In all the confusion of opening day, no one would help him. Then someone suggested he go home, so he did. He was not a very bright boy; he had not done very well as a freshman, and now he was two weeks behind in every subject. No one would help him—

Essential Mathematics Class

Essential mathematics class was difficult to control, and there were many times when I would have liked to have been able to knock a few heads together; it was difficult to teach because some students had trouble understanding the simplest operations. Nevertheless, I liked the students. There were times when they would work very hard, and I was so delighted that I could have hugged them.

And they were so quotable! When I gave them an inventory test on arithmetic operations with whole numbers, one said, "Ah, Miss Gloden," (I was single then), "this is easy. We may be dumb, but we're not stupid!" And when I was giving one of my biweekly lectures on the necessity of bringing pencil and paper to class, and threatening two of the worst offenders with being sent to the counselor's office, a third party protested, not quite under his breath, "But they don't sell pencils down there."

My most vivid impressions of this class centered around Joey. In September I had received a little card saying he was assigned to my class, but a week passed without my seeing him. His homeroom teacher had "blocked" him; this meant that he could not return to school until his parents came with him.

Finally he arrived, a short freshman boy of Spanish descent, with a winning smile and a crafty look in his eyes. He had a way of not hearing when I raised my voice, which forced me to be calm with him at all times—not an easy task! The trouble with Joey was that he could do mathematics but was too undisciplined to work for any length of time. And in a science room where most of the equipment was sitting on the back counter, there were any number of things a boy could find to play with. A tuning fork. *Ring.* "Put that away, Joey." "It wasn't *me,* Miss Gloden." (This in a hurt voice.) *Ring.* "Put that *away,* Joey." "Aah, you always blame me!" Sulk. A drawer full of corks of all sizes. "I want every cork picked up off the floor before you leave this class." He picked up the corks; this giving him an opportunity to walk around. A roll of twine. "Joey, what *are* you doing?" Joey slowly walking around the first row of lab tables, one end of the twine tied to his ankle, a sheepish grin on his face. The obvious solution was to put him at a front table. This helped, but did not completely thwart such an inventive boy.

The major battle between us was his aversion to bringing pencil and paper to class. I would lend pencils if something were given as collateral, and he usually had a pen, so that part of the problem was solved. One day in a moment of sheer desperation I said, "Say, Joey, I have an idea. Why don't I buy a pack of paper and bring it to class. Then you can pay me for it. I'll bring it every day, and you won't have to remember." I really thought that he would jump at the chance—but he was insulted! He got very serious and said, "I'll bring paper tomorrow." He did, to my delight, and I praised him. I guess my suggestion had been too much for his pride.

This lasted for about a week. Then he not only forgot to bring paper, but began cutting classes. When he returned after being blocked, he had a folder full of paper. This lasted two weeks, until Pete ripped the folder in two and Joey ripped it into quarters. This was all done very calmly, the first rip occurring by accident, and the second by design. It was not "cool" to carry paper and books around, and Joey wanted to be "cool." Then he bought a package of paper, and I brought it to class with me each day. So much for his pride.

Scores on his tests were among the best in the class. He was an intelligent boy, but very immature. He could usually grasp an idea rapidly, but needed to be told time after time to get busy, or to keep working. If he could not understand immediately, it was a real battle to have him try again. In my wanderings about the room to give individual help, I would frequently call without looking up, "Joey, how many do you have done now?"

Although the class was quiet in earlier meetings, by the end of the first month this was changing. I tried a new seating arrangement, which helped for that day; but the class was chaos again in two days. I felt that two things restricted the possibility of constructing an effective seating chart. The first was that no matter what I did the room would still be too crowded. I had forty students in a thirty-two seat room; allowing for absenteeism, this put about five people in folding chairs in the aisles. The second was that there were two students who spoke only Spanish and sat with bilingual classmates. I was consoled by the fact that I would lose some people in the leveling process, a complicated manipulation attempting to equalize class sizes by redistributing students. Using program cards of students in an overloaded class, the office tried to rearrange some schedules so that a few students could be put into another math class of the same kind without overloading other subjects. I knew that this process had begun for essential math, since one class had been taken up with filling out program cards.

That day's class was a total loss. It began badly with my selling graph paper, two sheets for a penny. I wanted the students to have it on short notice, so had decided to sell it myself. I should have had two students do it for me, because while I was being saleslady, a fight nearly started. One of the boys had been a problem to me from the beginning because he talked constantly. On the previous day I had moved him next to Jack, one of the quietest, most industrious boys in the class—also short-tempered, as it turned out. Anyway, Jack took a swing at Jim, and Jim had to be moved to another seat. So much for that particular attempt to change the seating chart.

Next a little girl from the office delivered the program cards with instructions to fill them out immediately, and I knew that all was lost. The cards were completed, amid varying levels of din, and six minutes remained in the period.

We discussed some ideas which were to serve as introduction for the next day's work, and I managed to restore some measure of quiet. What this meant was that I finally got all the wanderers settled and most of the conversation stopped.

When the leveling was done, this class was reduced to twenty-nine. This was still too many for the kind of individual help I wanted to give, but was a vast improvement over the original situation. I lost one troublemaker, Jim, and was left with two, Joey and Dave. I was glad to see Jim go, and hoped that one of the others would also become someone else's headache; but the two remained with me.

The leveling process had a surprising effect on my afternoon algebra class. Some of the best contributors had been taken, leaving an inattentive group. I had to adjust to an entirely new class personality, and could not understand why only three or four people could make such a difference. Then I realized how often I had been calling on the same people. Of course I had not had perfect attention before, but had ignored the chatter when the response from the others was adequate.

The following class description was all too typical:

"The students had docilely accepted my explanation of subtraction of integers, so I asked if they could explain to the 'man on the street' why $-5 - 3$ was not -2. Then some decided it was -2, and the battle began. People volunteered to come to the board to explain their positions; it was wild, and I thought it a worthwhile experience. But attention has been very bad ever since."

Sadly, attention was never very good, and the problem was worse in the essential math class. On most days that class sounded like an elementary school classroom: I repeated so many phrases and told so many people to stop talking and reminded so many people to get to work. I was embarrassed when anyone from the administration visited my class, because if one defined "control" as the ability to intimidate a student by a look or a word, I had none. I seldom raised my voice; nobody was afraid of me. About half of my students turned in homework regularly, and the percentage increased in those units which were entirely new material. But mine was not an orderly classroom, and this bothered me. My repertoire contained only one in-class punishment, and that was to send the offender to stand in the back of the room.

The atmosphere I had tried to create was friendly; the students were intimidated by the subject, so I tried to build their confidence. But here is where I ran into trouble—by the twentieth week some of them were feeling too comfortable. Two of the girls who did most of the assignments during the first grading period were doing very few during the second. I was not yet able to keep track of everybody while helping individuals, so some of them were wasting much time. I announced that I was going to subtract one point for each zero in my record, and this upset a few.

This class atmosphere spawned the first fight I ever stopped. Near the end of the period, four of the girls who sat in the back were talking, and from the expressions on two of the faces, I knew that something was wrong. I walked over as the bell rang, but nobody would tell me anything, and all left the room for their next classes. I returned to my desk to gather my things when I heard shouting in the hall and saw a crowd of students outside the door. As I rushed out, Mary and Cathy's shouting match became a shoving match; so I grabbed one girl, and someone else restrained the other. I talked to Cathy for ten minutes until she was more calm, then sent her to the counseling office with a note explaining the incident. The counselor talked to both girls, and they were friends again the following day.

There were several reasons why this was one of the most upsetting incidents of my first year. In the first place, it was the first fight I had witnessed since I was a freshman in high school, and that had involved two boys; I do not remember ever having seen girls fight before. I was afraid that the trouble would continue after school and involve the friends of each; this was compounded by the fact that one girl was white and the other was black. Even though this had nothing to do with the cause of the dispute, it would certainly worsen the character of any continuation of the disturbance in a school where there were many racial tensions beneath the surface.

I went to my next class in a daze, trying desperately to stop my knees from shaking and to concentrate on the lesson. My nonviolent, pacifistic nature was greatly shaken by the sight of two girl students screaming at one another with such hatred, especially since both were from my class. By the end of the period I had regained my composure.

At the end of the year this incident looked as trivial as it really was, and I was amazed that I had been so deeply affected by it, even for a time. Perhaps my second experience hardened me to this kind of thing.

This second frightening experience was another fight, this time in study hall. As far as I knew, Ben had never been a trouble-maker, so the incident caught me completely off guard. I had taken roll and was sitting at the desk. Bill finished writing the absence notices and walked over to the old cabinets at the front of the room. He was returning to the desk, an old newspaper in hand, when Ben rose from his front-row seat and confronted him. Angry words were exchanged, and Bill was knocked to the floor by a shove at the chest. I had risen in disbelief at the first words, thinking, "Great—what will I do *now*—overpower him myself?" I remember saying, "Ben—for heaven's sake, Ben, stop it." With Bill on the floor, Ben sat down; then he jumped to his feet again, shaking with rage, and turned toward the back of the room, as the other boy who usually helped me came forward. As Bill got up, I grabbed him and said, "Go down to the office and get help *fast!*" Bill left and I looked at Ben in time to see him shove my other helper down the aisle with enough force to send his glasses flying. "Ben, Ben—" I said quietly, walking toward him. Other students had risen from their seats; I felt I had to get him out of the room before any more students were involved. "Ben, are you coming with me?" I said, foolishly leaving the opening for a nega-tive response. He turned with arm raised (the aide later said that she thought he was going to hit me, but that thought never crossed my mind), nodded his head, and ran from the room, down three flights of stairs, and waited for me at the second floor. On the way down I tried to find out why he had done such a thing. He said he had wanted "to get those guys" for a long time. "They get away with things nobody else can get away with—like yesterday."

I remembered that the day before, the two helpers and a third boy had been throwing an eraser in the front of the room, while I was taking attendance. I had to tell them several times to stop.

Ben now said, "I was just waiting for one of them to hit me." His anger had been festering since at least yesterday, and possibly before. I found it strange that it was not directed at me, since I was at fault if anyone was being given preferential treatment.

We told our story to the vice-principal; Ben corrected me only once, and the vice-principal decided that Ben should report to her during third period. She told me later that he had been in trouble many times before and that he was showing other signs of instability. A few days later he signed out of school, at the school's insistence. I was not sorry to see him go, but I was sorry to realize that he would probably never be given the help he needed so badly. He needed psychiatric care of some kind, but his family was poor. I saw him once as I was leaving school; he was leaning against a car, talking to some other boys. I wondered what would become of him.

I had not been nearly so frightened this time, but I was shaken by the lack of motive. I had never seen anyone so angry for no apparent reason. I was astounded that I had remained so calm and that I had succeeded in stopping him. Instinctively I had done the right thing.

The Second Semester

In February I experienced my first real change in attitude. I began to dislike my classes, responding to their questions with irritation. I found that I had no more patience with their misbehavior. Curiously, I was still bereft of an arsenal of punishments, and resorted to the verbal correction and seat changes of previous use, while I seethed inwardly at my own impotence. For the first time I felt concern for the amount of material my algebra classes would cover—I began to doubt that we would reach quadratic equations. What had once appeared to me as a comfortable pace commensurate with student ability was now seen as an often wasteful, nearly slipshod use of valuable, unrecoverable time. And my once earnest students were now lazy and stupid.

February was also a time when I could not tolerate any of my colleagues, and I purposely avoided as many of them as I could. Everybody and everything upset me, and I wondered why the students who liked school did so, and silently agreed with the ones who did not.

Time took care of this problem, but not without a conscious effort to put anything related to school out of my mind as soon as I left the building. I simply refused to take anything home— no correcting of homework, no grading of tests, no preparation. Everything I did was accomplished during school time, or not at all. Gradually I recovered my sense of humor and assessed my position as being someplace between the sunny days of October and the long cold nights of February. I was not great, but neither was I totally ineffective. I began to plan further ahead and to try to anticipate difficulties. After a time I was able to view the ills of the school with more reason and less emotion and at least converse with other faculty members again. But February had been a lonely, frustrating time in which I had despaired of myself, the students, the school.

Study hall had progressed in an undistinguished fashion after the incident with Ben. It was not quiet, but I resigned myself to a certain degree of noise. Then in late March came a power struggle.

The bell was hard to hear on the top floor even when the room was quiet, and the clocks had never worked, so there was a degree of uncertainty surrounding our daily dismissal from study. This circumstance had generated a number of self-appointed clockwatchers who informed me that it was 11:23 by saying, "Bell rang." I foolishly ignored this, until one day "Bell rang" sounded five minutes early, and study hall emptied immediately.

The next day they tried it again, and I shouted, "The bell did *not* ring. Sit *down*. We are *due* in here until 11:23, and we will *stay* in here until 11:23." They sat down again; there was scattered applause, and I continued, "Yesterday we left five minutes early and that is not going to happen again."

The following day at 11:10 I announced, "I'd like to remind you that we are due in here until 11:23." No one said "Bell rang" and no one left early. We left on time every day after that, a fact which built up my confidence, even though the room was never particularly quiet.

Discipline problems took a strange twist in study hall. Having two brothers, I am used to trading comments with young men. Instinctively I responded to these boys in the same way. As a result there were times when one of them would push it too far. One day Jim ended an exchange with "Aw, Miss Gloden" and punched me on the arm. I was embarrassed and did not know how to react—should I overlook it, speak to him (what should I say?), or send him to his counselor? I tried to think of what another teacher would do in my position, and could not imagine it happening to anyone else. This business of touching people is very tricky, and I was as afraid of over-reacting as I was of not reacting in a way that would put a stop to further incidents of this type. What I said was, "Ah, Miss Gloden, nothing—don't forget I'm a teacher," in a serious, friendly, unshocked tone.

This raised all manner of questions about the image I was projecting; it was unthinkable that such a thing could happen to any of the teacher-images I knew. What was lacking in mine? I had not made an effort to start these chatter-sessions; I was not courting the student's favor; and I was trying not to play favorites. Still, I was getting a response to a signal I did not know I was sending.

Part of the difficulty was that I looked about nineteen, and I was friendly. I tried being more distant, and that made an impression—they thought I was angry with them! However, that incident was the last, so I suppose they got the message.

The death of Dr. Martin Luther King, Jr. was the occasion for crisis at our school, although the reactions were mild compared with others in the city. Friday was shock and sorrow walking; students cried; taps was played after homeroom, and a minute of silence was observed, a silence in which you could have heard a pin drop throughout that big old building. A memorial display appeared in the main corridor display case; plans for an assembly were begun. But tension and apprehension also walked; white students and teachers grew nervous as the grief sought expression. Black students gathered, threatened to walk out, talked with the administration. Classes were dismissed for the day. Confusion among the faculty was apparent at a meeting held that afternoon, a long chaotic meeting of impassioned statements which made two ideas manifest: the tension which had been building all year was now confronting everyone in a way which could not be ignored; the faculty was split on the issue of teacher authority and relationship with students. The question which lingered was "What do we do now?"

During the following week of scattered attendance and student demonstrations, the thing I felt most was inadequacy. I could not say anything to my students that would help; I was glad I was not in the inner city because I would have been even more useless there. The best I could be was sympathetic; I took my cue from my classes and did math only when it seemed a necessary return to a routine that offered security; I did not force anyone to participate. The following week my classes were as they had been before. But the school had changed—the students were recognized, however reluctantly, as a force to be reckoned with; but no one knew what form this reckoning would take.

In a second faculty meeting, a proposal for a student-faculty council was discussed, and divisions within the faculty were open. Briefly, the plan was to have four faculty members elected by the faculty and four faculty members elected by the students; eight students would be elected by the student body. Anyone who volunteered—faculty or student—was eligible.

Most of the men were threatened by this proposal: "No student is going to judge me." "Liberal" became a dirty word. The issue became "Who's running this school, the students or the teachers?" Somehow the proposal passed, after what seemed like days of heated debate.

I felt a bit strange for several days afterwards, surprised by the virulence around me. But it was then two months till the end of school, and as if in anticipation of this welcome event, things began to settle down. Even my classes began to improve.

Joey seemed better behaved in May, but perhaps I had just become used to him. He particularly liked doing things that needed some real thought and not simply rote skills. When we worked with open sentences, he was very clever and contributed frequently to class. Three other students had decided that his solution to the problem of bringing paper to class was the best one possible, so now I had four little packs of paper which I brought with me each day. There were still days (perhaps once a week, or at least once every two weeks) when I was driven nearly to tears by their inattentiveness. I do not understand why I did not break up the groups of talkers, but after a year of moving students around, the seating chart remained the same during the last two months.

In the middle of May, during the afternoon algebra class, I finally exploded, an event which accomplished what three calm sendings of students to the counselor had not. I had been irritated by the classes' lack of preparation, and when I asked an extraordinarily simple question of one of the talkers and he was unable to answer, it was too much. I threw the piece of chalk I had been holding with such force that it splattered all over the front of the room. *"Will* you pay attention! I get *so* irritated with you people," I muttered in a voice trembling with suppressed rage. Dead silence. The effect remained, and I never again had great problems with the worst offenders in that class. I had thrown out the seating chart in the beginning of May and announced that they could sit wherever they pleased, but that if they talked I would move them. It worked very well with the average talker, but made the taking of roll more difficult. After *thirty* weeks, I finally had control over that class.

I never succeeded in motivating them, however. Undone assignments, lack of participation, dull-eyed looks from the students—all these made me work harder, but with little effect.

My morning algebra class remained a joy to the end: alert, vocal, hard-working. A clear-eyed view must acknowledge the existence of students in this class whom that description does not fit, but their presence did not dim the general effect of the others.

By year's end three major concerns had evolved: discipline, concern with which had been amorphous at the beginning and more specific as the year progressed; motivation, always a concern but now viewed from a different perspective; and self-concept, a part of the other two and altered considerably during the year.

Discipline: I had walked into my classroom with the conviction that if I were fair, firm, and consistent, I would have little trouble with discipline. I still think that those qualities are essential, but they are insufficient. My discipline problems were not of the conspiratorial "Get the teacher" ilk, the cruel games that children play to torment their teachers. But in attempting to be fair, I often crossed the boundary between patience and over-tolerance; in retrospect I can judge incidents not on their own effects but as part of a pattern. Misbehavior which was minor at the time became a real problem when multiplied by 200 days; I was too tolerant of much nonsense. I really believe, however, that no one could have adequately warned me of this, that I had to experience this chain of trivial incidents so that I would have a standard for the future. We all wasted incredible amounts of time; I had too many sore throats; the quiet students suffered unnecessarily because of the repeated little background conversations that became part of the fabric of my classes and study hall.

What does being firm really mean? Certainly the notion of

standing behind a decision is part of it. If I ask Jeff to move, then Jeff must move. But here I encountered another difficulty—my concept of firmness meant repetition of the initial request, *ad nauseum*. I had failed to consider my course of action if the request were not met. Actually, I was much better in this regard before I knew the students well enough to become involved with personalities. Sure, Louis is a nice boy; sure, his behavior is not really terrible; and sure, it is going to make him feel bad when I say, "See me after class," but I could no longer afford to let him get away with his misbehavior. I needed to develop an arsenal of in-class techniques for control, and this realization is far distant from the things-will-take-care-of-themselves attitude with which I entered the school.

Motivation is related to discipline, but my perception of this relationship has changed. At first I thought that all one had to do was to motivate people properly and there would be no discipline problems. That is partly true. But I had underestimated the enormity of the task of motivation. Motivation was a once-and-for-all kind of step, in my mind: students were unmotivated, then the skillful teacher motivated them. I did not see this question as the day-to-day problem which it is, nor did I operate from the assumption that my students did not really care about math. I always tried to make my classes interesting, but that judgment was made from the viewpoint of someone who liked it. Motivation was an issue only at the beginning of the year, I had thought; and when it still existed in February, I was frustrated and angry.

The glowing self-confidence I had had at the beginning of the year was based on my knowledge of mathematics, my concern for persons as individuals, and my desire to teach. I no longer see myself in that way. Some day I may be as good a teacher as I thought I would be in September, but I have much more to learn from experience. I need more skill in adapting my mathematical knowledge to the high school level; I need to ask good questions and to throw more of the thinking in class onto the students; I need to give more illuminating explanations of questions raised by students. My concern for the individual must better balance my concern for the group; my intellectual awareness of the value and necessity of punishing children for misbehavior must find more effective expression in practice.

In the matter of discipline, I have used techniques which were effective when used by my teachers on me. But I was a docile, earnest student, who liked school and teachers. What had been appropriate and sufficient disciplinary measures for me were completely ineffective when applied to some of my students.

The Last Days

On Friday of the last full week of school, one of my classes surprised me with a party. They had been most interested in my wedding plans, where I would be living the following year, and whether I would continue to teach. But I did not expect such an expression of appreciation. As I began class, a little procession entered the room: one girl bearing napkins and a knife, a second with a large sheet cake on which had been written "Congratulations, Miss Gloden," and a third with a beautifully wrapped package. I was overwhelmed! I began cutting cake for everyone; but then they got impatient about the gift, so two girls took over the cake while I fumbled with the package. The card had been signed by everyone in the class and accompanied a beautiful cream-and-sugar set. In the middle of the party, the fire-drill bell sounded, and there was a moment of uncertainty about where to hide the goodies; but one of the tall boys put my present on the top of the bookcase, and the cake was hastily covered—since there was a principal's directive against parties, we all felt such precautions were absolutely necessary! In all respects, it was a lovely party and one of the nicest things that had ever happened to me. I was very grateful to those students for their kindness.

From that point until the end of school, my spirits steadily declined. The last day of classes was a farce: I was through, the students had "tuned me out" the preceding Friday, and so we took it easy. In the algebra classes I discussed each student's grades with him, and each of them wrote about the year—what they had enjoyed best and least, and suggestions for the future. Typically, in the morning class nearly all completed the questionnaire; in afternoon class, about half.

On records day we entered final grades in course books and record cards, computed promotions and attendance figures, recorded failures on the counselor's list and successes on the lists that went to the principal and the honor clubs. Even though I had an excellent student helper, I was at school until late afternoon; I was so terribly slow.

Friday was greeted with weary relief. I was desperately tired of the school and everything related to it. It was as though the last ounce of energy had been expended on the previous day, in tediously recording all those wretched little letters and numbers, reducing the thirty students in my homeroom to a code so important and so meaningless. We said our good-byes—they all knew that I would not be returning, that I was being married in July and was going to another state to teach—some sought me out to copy down my new address, amid promises to write. (As expected, they never did, but it was a nice gesture.)

I thought I would be sad to leave my students, as I had been when I was student teaching. But a year of total responsibility is much more wearing than three months of partial responsibility. I was not at all unhappy to be leaving. I needed the approaching summer, away from school and students and teachers, to sort out my experiences and to try to identify the things I felt intuitively that I had learned. I was looking forward to the fall, a new beginning where I would be a better teacher for my year's experience. But most of all I was glad to be finished—the first year was over, at last! Good-bye school; good-bye people I liked; good-bye people I disliked; good-bye without regret.

Wylie Crawford

The Other Side of the Coin

After a full week of teacher orientation workshops, I made my teaching debut in one of the most remarkable public schools in the country. I had just finished a year of study at the University of Chicago and was ready to try out some of the theories and dime-store philosophies that I had come across during the past year. One of these, my favorite, was that teaching was simply the other side of the coin from studying. Every student has a pretty well-formed idea of what makes a good teacher, and I was no exception. All those memories of good and bad times in the classroom as a student should provide a beginning teacher with a wealth of information about his new job. All that I had to do was to stick to those hallowed memories during the upcoming year and not let them get clouded over by the other pressures that would inevitably come to me. If I could do this, I felt sure I would come out all right in June. In addition to this and other less significant notions, I was fortunate enough to approach my teaching year with a bit more confidence than some of my peers, since I had already had a taste of teaching (not to mention a taste of surrogate parenthood) while at a boarding school in Switzerland. There I was teacher, father, and all-around buddy to about 100 students. I had begun to learn some of the basic techniques of the "ed biz"—how to present difficult subject matter in plain talk, the art of the ad lib, how much preparation is required for a "presentation" (and how much is excessive), et cetera. As it turned out, these would not be prime concerns in my new situation.

One of the first sources of confusion in my new job was the organizational structure of the school. After a week of orientation discussion in and around various topics pertinent to the "innovative" school, I was clear as to how things should work; but as the weeks passed I became more concerned with how they actually *did* work. The school is a lower-middle-class suburban public school which employs various innovative techniques in order to achieve the personal development of both the students and the teachers. In order to do this, it allows considerable flexibility in the use of facilities, course scheduling, and study requirements. It was one of the first schools to use the "Trump Plan," a scheme which divides the school week into 100 twenty-minute "modules." Classes may be any multiple of these modules, determined by teachers' requests. The schedule for the 1400 students and 70 teachers is created by computer, and recycles weekly, instead of daily.

The school also employs a tracking system. A student's track is a function of the subject he is taking. He may be in the A-track (advanced) in math, in the B-track (average) in science, and in the C-track (remedial or slow learner) in social studies. Any student (with parental permission) may initiate a change in his own track whenever he wishes, except that he is not generally permitted to drop to a track lower than his ability level.

All courses in the school comprise four phases of instruction—and these will be mentioned later, "Class," so please take note.

1. Large-group instruction. Meetings (in the auditorium) during which all students enrolled in a course gather to hear a conventional lecture or up-to-date "media presentation" on topics "not readily found in outside reading."
2. Seminars. Groups of about a dozen students which meet with the teacher to discuss current material. These are often chaired by the students themselves.
3. Laboratories. Sessions of about twenty students patterned after the conventional task-oriented science labs. These labs are adapted to all subjects, however.
4. Independent study. Replacing the conventional study hall, this

is time during which the student's schedule is blank (between thirty and forty percent of his schedule). I.S. areas are set up by each subject field. These areas contain study carrels, displays, and a library. The resource materials (filmstrips, books, tapes, and special equipment) are handled by a clerk who also does occasional paper-grading and routine work for teachers. In addition, the cafeteria and senior lounge are also available to students during their blank time.

While the school stresses the development of the individual, it also uses team teaching. Each subject field has its own team of teachers which collectively determines the overall requirements and curriculum for the field. The work load is divided up according to the members' desires and backgrounds. This usually results in two to four teachers on each grade level (of about 300–400 students). Thus, under team teaching, all teachers are ultimately responsible for all students. At first, the concept of team teaching may seem contradictory to the goals of individualized instruction and the development of the individual. In practice, it is not contradictory at all. A student is likely to get better individualized instruction when he can choose to deal with one of several teachers than when he is stuck with the same one for a whole year. Development of the individual teacher is painfully illustrated under team teaching when a group of people sits down and tries to agree upon how and what to teach the students. At times like these, the place seems more like a teacher-training institution than a public high school.

To me, however, the most remarkable aspect of the school's operation is not that it uses the techniques just described, but that administratively it is a normal public high school, subject to the whims of a school board, and attended by the students in the district. This school is unlike, and in stark contrast to, many private institutions which "stack the deck" by admitting only selected bright students who would undoubtedly fare well no matter what kind of school they found themselves in. Team teaching, individualized instruction, and the "Trump Plan" are not worth much, after all, unless they can be used with success in the "average" school community.

Aside from these structural-organizational concerns, I was apprehensive about the whole subject of control of large quantities of potentially hostile students. My past experience offered no illumination on this account. The students in the Swiss school had been few in number and dependent on the teachers for much more than mere instruction, and so discipline problems were unheard of. All I had to go on at the onset of this year, then, were such experiences as are described in the popular literature; e.g., *To Sir, With Love, Up the Down Staircase* and *The Blackboard Jungle*. These obviously fictionalized accounts of new teachers' adventures in high school seemed to present realistic discipline problems, but the resolutions of these problems seemed either over-idealized, incomplete, or inappropriate to my own temperament. In addition, the schools described were inner-city schools, which my school was not. A previous visit to the school had indicated that the students here were the sons and daughters of suburban blue-collar workers, somewhat like the "mini-hoods" of my own high-school days, but hardly knife-toting delinquents.

How was I going to talk to them? Could I be relaxed and a "pal"? Or an authoritarian and hard-nosed dictator? I doubted if I could pull off the latter, and certainly the former seemed more in keeping with the school's philosophy.

I had resolved ahead of time that the best method at first would be to establish myself as a "significant other," that is, someone to be reckoned with. This seemed to be necessary. Past experience as a student had shown me that teachers who were not "significant others" were not effective in maintaining either student attention or interest. They were teachers who had been judged unworthy of respect either through their weakness, their injustice, or their ignorance of subject matter. On the other hand, the teachers I held as superior models had found several diverse ways of maintaining this desirable status. My own high school biology teacher, for example, treated us almost as if we were college freshmen. I wish I could see him in action again, as I have probably forgotten many of his better techniques, but I do remember some of them (as well as a lot of biology, which I was determined to dislike). He enjoyed words and punned with many of the terms we had to remember, thus making them more memorable. He gave no routine "cook-book" assignments, but published a schedule of topics to be covered and introduced us to the judicious use of the index. From then on, we had the impression of being on our own in the course. He treated us as adults, and after a while, we responded accordingly.

As another example, my physics teacher used to break the classroom tension (or boredom) with occasional stories about his (imaginary) menagerie of pet monsters which he kept "back in the cave" (along with his wife). No one wanted to get on his bad side, for fear of depriving us all of his stories.

I approached the first days of class with all these preconceptions floating around in my mind, and with a mixed bag of emotions (and undescribable gastric distress attributable to the long drive to school, the early homeroom, and the first days). Chaos threatened during the first week or so. About two-thirds of the staff were new teachers, and the students usually knew what was happening much better than we did. At the same time, the large nucleus of newcomers also had the effect of disorienting the students enough to keep problems down to a tolerable level. My team-mate and I found ourselves responsible for about 300 juniors in the upper two tracks of science. The A-track consisted of a physics course, while the B-track, designed by last year's teaching staff (who were, for the most part, at other schools) was a general science course involving topics from atmospheric pollution to Zinjanthropus, from theories of housing to parapsychology. The physics course was not too much trouble, since physics was my major field in college. Most of my initial activities in physics involved making up a course outline for the next month and selecting the best references for each topic. The general science was another story, however. Hours were spent in trying either to comprehend or to create materials for this course. Throughout the year, it was a continual race to keep ahead of the students in these varied and unfamiliar topics. As a result, it was not until well into October that I found enough time or energy to devote to the more personal and rewarding activities of the teacher: talking to students and other teachers during free time, sitting back and looking at where I was going, and making connections between 300 names and 300 people in front of me. The latter was no mean task. The traditional name-learning aids used in other schools unfortunately were not available here. A seating chart (for the large-group instruction) was made up, but was too big to be useful, and there were no fixed seats in the other activities (labs, seminars, independent study). Students met during the week in varying combinations and at irregular intervals, so that some students were very familiar and others were nearly anonymous. After a while, of course, most of the names became associated with faces, but this process took longer than it would have in a traditional school. The names, I might add, were learned just in time. I had the majority of them down pat just as I realized that my control problems were beginning to show.

In the beginning, my fears about discipline and class control were abated. Instead of finding students who were organized for an all-out, massed offensive, I found students who wished for the most part to be left alone; instead of finding students who were outspoken and arrogant, I found students who were yielding and eager not to "make waves." For the first week or two, the vast majority of my students just sat, seemed to listen attentively, and asked questions when called for. All was sweetness and light, it seemed—except that, at times, I felt like a leper. As I walked through the halls or independent study areas, I was aware that I was being "sized up." I was being regarded with sidelong glances —both curious and fearful—which seemed to ask: "Is he an axe-murderer or just a child-strapper?" This was somewhat disarming, since my idea of becoming a "significant other" was to have the class feel at home with me and like me, so that if the going ever got rough during the year, I would be able to recall the pleasant days, when we were all friends, and emotionally black-mail them into wanting things that way again. But this approach couldn't work, of course, if they were convinced from the start that I was another ogre just like those of their grade school days. It seemed that the fact that I wore a suit and tie made me a tyrant, ready to beat them if they looked cross-eyed. I was deter-mined to win them over by personality, however, contrary to the advice from one of the more experienced (and cynical) teachers who warned: "Don't smile until Christmas."

My colleague's advice was not taken, of course, since my ideal classroom was one in which everyone was happy, where every-one felt free to speak out when he had something important to say, without fear from harsh criticism or ridicule from me or from his fellows. To create such a situation, it was only natural to smile, and so I did. And eventually, the class did too, but in a slightly different way. As the first month passed, the routine and boredom of even this school began to set in. Many of the stu-

dents did not understand why they were required to take four
years of science (or English, or physical education, for that matter). The happy, relaxed, loosely disciplined class which I saw
developing began to take strange and subtle turns in the wrong
directions. The students were not just happy and relaxed, they
were content and almost asleep. I started to get the message:
their natural curiosity had not been aroused. I tried to spice up
my presentations and asked more questions of individuals in the
class, but this seemed to no avail. The symptoms persisted—one
student would be looking out the window; another student would
be sitting on a table when there were chairs still available; two
girls would be gossiping just a little too loud, and would continue
even when I approached and finally stood right next to them.
While these were noticeable changes, no one of them was ob-
jectionable enough to make a big fuss about. After all, my own
concept of the ideal classroom atmosphere was broad enough to
allow for occasional disinterested students. There would be days
when they, too, would become involved and some other students
would lose interest. Besides, in the cosmic view of things, the
state of the world today was not going to hinge on the fact that
a few minor infractions were tolerated occasionally. Treating the
students as adults, I felt that they knew they were pushing my
patience a bit and that a gentle reminder would be sufficient to
set things straight. And it did, for a while. But soon I found
myself giving mild admonishments more' and more often, and
always to the same small group of offenders. Now, instead of
just looking out the window, they were waving to passing cars
while my back was turned. Instead of just sitting on the tables,
a few were sprawled out on them. My resolve was still not shaken.
They would soon tire of such shenanigans, and I could win them
back through my artfully-designed presentations. After all, I had
expected much worse, and we were still getting used to each other.
When they saw the folly of it all, our little testing period would
be over.

   In reality, as far as the students were concerned, the testing
period was already over, and they had won the game. I was going
to be a pushover. And, since the other students had been watching the events of the first month, my list of offenders got longer
as my blood pressure got higher. The situation got to the point
where I had to brace myself before walking into certain particu-

larly "liberated" classes. On the days that I gave myself no pre-game pep talk, I would come out of the session blaming myself for not having done enough to control the situation. I felt I had very little idea of what I could ever turn that class into. But one day when I was not mentally braced for the usual harassments, I did what came naturally and gave it to them with both barrels—a thorough chewing-out. I'm sure it was too emotional (yet at the same time too apologetic—I suspected that it was my own vagueness that had let things go this far), but it worked. A month before, I would have considered it an unnecessary act, and a sign of failure. But now, it seemed the only thing to do for my own peace of mind. I had been poisoned and insulted by their giggles and inattentions long enough, and I had begun to blame myself for not being able to stand it any longer or to stop it entirely.

After this incident, I felt that things would simmer down, which they did for a while. But when trouble began to brew again, I asked each individual in the little core group of five to meet me after school for a five-minute conference. All agreed to come, but only one showed up. I was obviously still not a "significant other" for them, in any sense of the word. The delinquent four received one-hour detentions, the first detentions I had given that year. I was not proud to have given them, but my patience and re-sources had run out. I was glad that this procedure was available to me, since I had dug myself such a deep hole that I needed some show of external authority to help me begin the return to sanity.

This was only a beginning. There were endless tests to my authority throughout the year. Somehow, my chosen initial ap-proach to classroom control seemed to extend my testing period indefinitely. Throughout the year I felt that I had to prove over and over again that I really was a teacher, and not just the good-natured boob I had seemed at the beginning of the year. It seemed that since I at first chose not to use the facial expressions, verbal barbs, and peer pressures that every "real" teacher uses, I could never use them effectively in the students' eyes. I concluded that for me to eventually "break the rules" and do what I really wanted to do with the class, I first had to learn those rules very well—well enough to become an instant veteran of the granite-faced club of beings who are forced to their conformity by past decades of still more granite-faced teachers. My general discomfort in my new role as disciplinarian, sage, and unwilling enemy of the student populace was heightened by what seemed for a long time to be a most disturbing phenomenon: the loss of my first name. At the same time, I was unsure how to address other adults in the school without offending them. The members of the science team were on a first-name basis from the first days, probably because most of us were young and in a new situation. But with the other teachers, especially the older ones, and even if I was fortunate enough to be able to recall their complete names, it was quite difficult to determine how they wished to be addressed. Even worse was the problem of the office help and the clerks. Originally, it seemed to me that they should be addressed just as familiarly as the teachers on the team, but I was rebuffed by them (so it seemed) and was continually called "Mr. Crawford" (shudder). Until this time, I had been known as "Mr. Crawford" only under the most unpleasant conditions—e.g., when addressed by an impatient professor or when applying for a job. I certainly was not comfortable with the name, when it came from adults. As it turned out, school etiquette dictated that I could expect to be addressed formally by staff women old enough to be my mother, presumably out of respect for the teacher's professional standing.

A curious permutation of this situation is that some of the teachers felt compelled to address each other as "Mr. _____" whenever students were within hearing distance. I actually heard one teacher apologize to another for having called him by his first name "in public." Fortunately, on the science team, this practice, dehumanizing and pretentious as it is, was abolished. We all agreed that the students knew our first names, after all, and that they probably wouldn't start "getting ideas" about calling us by these names. I suspected they had some better nicknames for us by now, anyway.

Surprisingly enough, two of my favorite students started showing me that my liking for them was ill-concealed by sneaking in an occasional "Thanks, Wylie" near the end of class, or while receiving papers. Although this was nothing serious enough to get upset about, I did feel the need to express some sort of displeasure, if only to maintain the impartiality and authority of the class situation. After some time, it felt natural to be called by my last name by the students, and I felt natural enough in rebuking those who did not do so.

Early in the year, while I was still touchy about the subject of proper forms of address, one student approached me after a seminar and timidly asked me how my first name was pronounced. Two weeks earlier I probably would have told him my full name with both barrels, "Wylie Crawford the Third," but in my newly-developed, well-braced manner I asked how he thought it might be pronounced. For a second it looked as if he might give up and go home, and I could have kicked myself. But he responded, "I don't—well, how *do* you pronounce it?" By this time I had returned to my senses and had realized that it was quite flattering for a student even to care how I pronounced my first name. After all, it wasn't such a big deal. So I told him gladly—"*Wy*-lee."

This incident represented in miniature what was happening to me. I had found myself in a very critical spotlight. I began to notice that everyone noticed me. Near the end of a class-period, for example, any movement on my part—the closing of grade books, gathering of materials, or peeking at the clock—would result in an attempted stampede for the door. Since the school has no bells to signal the passing of classes, someone has to keep his eye on the clock. The teacher has the choice of either doing his own clock-watching (which arouses the students) or trusting the students to do it for him (which results in ever-shorter classes). In the same vein, any pause in a fast-paced, exciting lecture (other than for dramatic emphasis or eye-to-eye discipline) will lead to quick and complete loss of attention from the students. All of which forces the teacher to watch himself much more closely than ever before. To involve the class, he must speak "teacherese" with mouth and mien. He must have a well-practiced repertoire of emotions, and not always be his casual, fun-loving, broad-minded self. The students seem to take on the atmosphere that the teacher creates, and a room full of casual, fun-loving, broad-minded selves is generally an impossible teaching or learning situation. The only problem was that while I was struggling to learn "teacherese," it was hard to step out of the role long enough for me to tell another human being how my name was pronounced.

One of the institutions in the school with which I agreed whole-heartedly but which I was temporarily unable to support was athletic eligibility. All students were required to "successfully participate" in mathematics, science, English, and social studies for all four high school years. Any student who was not "successfully participating" in at least three of these subjects was barred from any athletics for the duration of his failure. As a result, every week I would receive a list of students enrolled in sports, with a request to determine if any of them were failing any of my courses. I would have been only too happy to comply with the request, but I encountered difficulty in deciding which, if any, of my students were actually failing—which brings me to the subject of grades.

The whole question of grades and their significance was a subject of confusion to many members of the science team. Never before had I realized that there were several different grading philosophies. I had long since heard the argument against grades and had decided that they were not so evil. But the idea of a "weighted grade" was unknown to me until then. Apparently, in some schools, the grade which is given the student on his report is adjusted before it is entered on his permanent record, depending on the difficulty of the course he has taken. Thus, under such a weighted system, a student getting an A in a remedial math course and a student getting a C in a calculus course, might both receive a B on their permanent records for some nondescript "mathematics" course. The rationale for this practice is that colleges rarely consider what courses the student takes, but rather depend on his rank in class or overall grade point average to determine his scholastic worth.

At our school, however, the policy has been to give a nonweighted grade to all students. This meant that a B was a B was a B, no matter what brand of science was being studied. After the first marking period it became clear that few of the new teachers understood this policy, for it was discovered that there were an excessive number of failures in the A and B tracks. The question that naturally arose was, how can a teacher be expected to compare a student's scientific savvy in, say, mechanics, with another's competence in general ecology. Even worse, since none of us had any contact with the students in the C-track, we were poorly qualified to judge the difference between a D and an F, since we had no idea how most of the students receiving these grades were doing. An experienced teacher, of course, has a better idea of the range of achievement of his students and is capable of grading any one student against a composite picture of all past classes. But I had no such scale to go by, and so had to rely on a somewhat mathematical approach. Since the science grades for all the juniors would theoretically yield the proverbial bell-shaped curve, and since by the junior year most students had presumably been placed in the right track, the vast majority of the C's should fall in the middle track. This group should also contain a moderate number of B's and D's and very few A's or F's. On any given test, then, the clump of students around the average score would receive a C. Medium-sized clusters above or below this C group would receive B's and D's. Then what about the stragglers? How far below the D-range would still be a D, and how far below would be an F? Here, we were told, the teacher could be subjective (as he is in all grading, after all). Well, after much soul searching, I was usually capable of justifying failing grades for students who really deserved them; but this was an unpleasant process, and the sort of thing that should only happen to a teacher once every few months, just in time for report cards. It should only be done when a complete curve can be constructed, when the other teachers teaching the course can add their students' grades to the graph. Returning to the problem of athletic eligibility, then, the idea of determining, each week, which of my students was failing was a near-impossibility. This situation caused me some grief for several months, until I realized that none of the students on the list were in any danger of failing, as shown by a curve of the first quarter's marks. After that, I felt justified in making an occasional check of the list to see that none of the two or three failing students that I had were in any athletics. I completed the year without handing in one ineligibility. In so doing, I probably saved myself countless broken car antennas.

Grading was not the only procedure under discussion this year, of course. The managing of the physics class, for example, was in a continual state of re-evaluation. My teammate had taught four years in another school, and I had, in addition to my year in Switzerland, done a year of observation in the University of Chicago's Laboratory School. Both of us were going to forget our past and start anew, however. With all that we had heard during teacher orientation week, we gathered that we could set up the ideal class from the start. We issued a monthly schedule of topics to be covered, along with a list of available or recommended sources. The lectures were given with the understanding that some outside reading had been done independently beforehand, so that at least the vocabulary would not have to be explained in class. Of course, I realized that at age sixteen, I would hardly have been able to do what we were asking our students to do. But, after all, our students were juniors in an ambitious school, and greater things were expected of them, what with all that unscheduled time and material available. In addition, the physics students were there because they had elected to take the course, so, naturally, untold quantities of motivation were in order.

I don't know why, but in those first few weeks, everything was seen and believed as if through rose-colored glasses. In any case, the glasses quite soon faded, and reality came glaring through. While the school was ambitious, the students were normal—very normal. True, the large-group lectures were intended to cover material that students could not get on their own from outside sources. In practice, the large groups should have been introductory all along, since the students found it nearly impossible to get anything at all from outside sources.

Eventually, the students became discouraged because of their lack of comprehension, and began to give up. The laboratory time, for example, was unscheduled, and so attendance was not taken. It soon became evident, however, that while most students turned in a lab write-up, only about half the class was actually coming in to do the experiments.

At this point, my team-mate and I disagreed on the cause of the problems. I felt that the material was too abstractly presented and was coming too hard and heavy for them to keep up with. Under these conditions, they could never get sufficiently interested in it to carry out satisfactory independent study work (one of my own college problems, I might add). He believed, on the other hand, that the school was not strict enough with the students and that they were therefore much lazier than those he had taught in the past (one of his own high school problems, he might have added). Although this difference of opinion came between us through the year, we both underwent considerable professional growth because of it and eventually compromised in each other's direction. The net result was quite good, showing that there probably was some truth in both views. We each attracted different kinds of students, and it seems to me that more students got involved in physics as a result of having two teachers than would have done so in a conventional class with a group of the same size.

Another aspect of the teacher's job was a feeling of responsibility for all phases of the students' growth—a school is expected to uphold the moral and social standards of the community. One day last year, some of the teachers were gossiping in the lunch room about the senior prom. One of them mentioned how comical it was to see "our young ladies" in heels, with their hair up, stunningly dressed, and as a final touch, jawing away on a piece of Dubble-Bubble gum. I have to admit that I can't recall seeing many people chewing gum at my own senior prom. In my proper, oh-so-clean-upper-middle-class school all rules were strictly enforced (or more accurately, rarely challenged). The reality of my new teaching situation was something else. Gum chewing in class was rampant. It was *the* thing for the girls to do. The sight of vast numbers of them grinding away, with mouths wide open and gum crackling, was awesome.

What, if anything, was I going to do about it? Aside from the fact that I was selfishly opposed to the practice, deploring the disfigurement of an otherwise attractive girl, there was a school rule involved which should be enforced as any other. The school handbook, generally a well thought-out and realistic document, said that "gum chewing is allowed only in the cafeteria and the senior lounge." This particular ruling seemed somewhat ludicrous when viewed through my newly adjusted, clear-lensed glasses. I am not familiar with its history, but I would be curious to know why the cafeteria and senior lounge were exempted from the prohibition. It would seem easier to enforce a regulation of this type if it were a general rule, applicable everywhere in the school. The prohibition on smoking, for example, covered all school property (which effectively limited it to the washrooms).

Anyway, I decided to enforce the rule, and in my inexperienced fashion, I did it on an individual basis—thereby guaranteeing myself another lesson in insanity and frustration. For the first few weeks I satisfied myself with stilling stray masticators by having them simply remove and discard the offending substances. But, alas, that was not enough to keep the problem under control. The lack of any punishment encouraged further offenses. While I felt sure, at the start, that my patience would hold sway, I soon saw that unless I was prepared to spend nearly all of my energies on this task, I could not possibly succeed. I had somehow expected that sooner or later the chewers would tire and, anticipating the inevitable, would kick the habit without my having to give any punishments. But the job was too big. Soon the desired results seemed less attractive than the peace which would be gained by giving up. Then the rationalizations set in: I was there to teach, not to police the students; gum chewing was not the worst thing in the world; I would do it right next year. Gum chewing is surprisingly easy to get used to.

As the year grew older, I discovered that I was being asked to spend too much time on what I considered useless tasks. These demands came not from the administration or other teachers, but from the students themselves. Somehow I had come to the job with the understanding that not only was my time available for the students to use, but also to abuse. Once I had gotten the idea that I was there to answer questions, it somehow didn't occur to me to select the questions I was going to answer. This was evidenced by my willingness, through some sort of numbness, to answer any and every question posed. A prime example of this, and one which aroused me from my numbness, occurred near the end of the year, when I announced the time and place of the general science final examination. Since this was important information, I gave it a large build-up. I waited until I had complete silence in the large-group session of 210 students. I told them that this was information that had to do with their final, which was just a week away, and I told them to copy down what I was going to write on the overhead projector. (This was the full treatment—they always wrote down everything that went on the projector.) I did this on Thursday. By Monday, students were already coming to me asking when the exam would be and where they should go to take it. Had they been in Thursday's large-group session? Yes, they had. At the beginning of the hour? Yes. Then why didn't they know the answer to their own questions? They had forgotten. Well, then, I recommended that they ask some student who had *not* forgotten to write it down. I undoubtedly spent more time telling them to ask other students for the information than I would have in telling it to them myself, but I was obstinate and out of patience. Just to see how far it all would go, I gave the information to the group once again in Tuesday's large-group session, making no mention about my annoyance with their irresponsibility. Still, on Tuesday, Wednesday, nay even on the day of the test, they were asking the same questions. It seemed to me that somehow I had failed during the year, and now I was reaping the bitter rewards. From now on, I decided, the rule was going to be: say it once; say it clearly and very, very slowly (in "teacherese"); and then tell yourself that everyone in the class who was worth anything at all had heard it. I have since noticed that teachers who follow this rule manage to get heard the first time. It may seem like a trivial rule, if not painfully self-evident; but somehow, in the confusion of emotions at the beginning of the year, I had gotten into some pretty bad habits.

On the brighter side, some things went quite smoothly. Conducting seminars was going to be, for me, the most important phase of the school's four-phase instruction. In practice, it was one of the most satisfying activities of the year. Several factors contributed to making the seminars enjoyable. First, by their very nature and size, they were easy to control. Second, the physics students were the ones who were scheduled in regular, stable seminars. Finally, the physics students were generally bright and/or confused enough to bring up questions of their own, which made the job more rewarding. It was as a result of their questions that I realized how little science background even the most intelligent and conscientious students had. (Hence the aforementioned argument with my teammate about what the problem was with the physics class.)

Way back at the beginning of the year, I saw all three of my physics seminars before I met with them in the large-group session. I had toyed with several ideas about what to do with our introductory seminars in order to set the tone of the year—ask for summaries about what they had done during the summer, what they wanted to do after they left high school, what their impressions and gripes were about the school. Most of these ideas struck me as trite and artificial, and at the last minute I decided to try to find out what they thought physics was all about, what they thought we were going to be doing this year, and what they had heard about the course. These subjects seemed to be the least boring of those I had considered, and they dealt with what interested *me* the most, anyway. I didn't want to spend the time talking *at* them, and except for occasional lapses, I didn't. One group asked about my college, since they were thinking about making out applications at that time. Eager to show how un–teacher-like I was, I obliged willingly, throwing in a few gripes that I had had about my own education. Later, we drifted onto the questions "What is science and what do we need it for? What is 'truth' in science?" Since most of the students had an opinion, we all got acquainted rather quickly and the first seminars passed painlessly. During the first part of the year, I used the seminars as testing grounds for my large-group lectures, trying to find out exactly what they knew so that I could develop an accurate estimation of what I could assume when giving explanations and presenting new material. This worked quite well and filled up my seminar topics for the first few awkward months while we all got used to each other. Later I tried introducing "task-oriented" seminars, with mixed success. (One of the better ones involved determining if a single piece of tinted plastic was polarized or not.) Of the three seminar sections, I was quite satisfied with the first two, and almost always dissatisfied with the third. The students in the third seminar were not the best in the class, and I might well have become stale by the time I got to them, having just finished the second seminar immediately before. But whatever the reason, we rarely seemed to get into a discussion which involved the group.

Seminars were expected to be challenging, and they were. Large-group sessions on the other hand, were expected to be routine; but they were hardly that. At first, the system seemed simple. Two teachers were assigned to large-groups. One was the surveyor of the group, taking attendance and admitting late-comers. The other, the person in the spotlight, was the lecturer, who was also responsible for "law and order." In practice, how-ever, he was often a teacher from another grade level, or even another teaching team, since the subjects covered were so varied. Being unfamiliar with the group, he was not always the best per-son to handle discipline. Now, since I was the one charged with attendance and was almost always present no matter who was lecturing, I was responsible for the conduct of the audience, as a sort of "back-seat driver." Once again I started off the year in a bind. Our philosophy of student responsibility, as I saw it, held that a student was not obliged to be an A student. As long as he was quiet and didn't bother those who wanted to hear what was going on, I had no bones to pick with him. In my naïveté, and coming from my background, I had no idea what situations might develop from such a philosophy. When I saw students not taking notes, I told myself (and them, on occasion) that it was all right. I cautioned them that, of course, they would run into trouble when the tests came along, but it was their privilege to flunk, if they chose to. Needless to say, I would encourage note-taking, but I would not demand it. By expressing this attitude, I had shown them once again that I was not a "real" teacher, but a push-over. Students began to try sprawling over the chairs, sleeping, and passing notes. When caught, they displayed expressions of utmost surprise. After all, they weren't disturbing any other students—it was their right to flunk. And there they had me, I had to admit. So I had to broaden their minds (and mine) with a more complete explanation: Their activities were likely to annoy and distract the lecturer, who would then give a poor lecture, thus hurting the other students. This seemed like a trumped-up explanation to them. It was the gospel truth to me. I had, by then, received several bitter complaints from fellow teachers who found my group unbearable. Although I felt it was up to the "spotlight man" to control the group, I had to admit that my group was a bit unruly. In any case, I was not permitted to sit calmly in the rear of the room, as I had imagined, drinking in the information being offered to the obedient and grateful masses of humanity. Instead, to atone for my earlier "broad-minded" laxity, I was obliged to spend most of the rest of the year proving to them that I meant what I said. If there is any single reason why I would like to teach again next year, it would be to right the wrongs of this year, to spend a year with a class exposed to my newly-formed idea of how a class should act. The results might still not live up to my first day's expectations, but at least I would have the satisfaction of seeing them a lot closer to that goal than they were this year.

As things have turned out, I will not be teaching next year, and won't get to try out my new attitudes right away. Instead, I expect to be working as a semi-administrator (on a half-time basis) in data processing. As the year progressed, and things began to settle down, it occurred to me that a computer could be used profitably to score objective tests. Since I had had some experience in programming at the university, I wrote a program to do this tedious work for my own classes. The program began to be used by other members on the science team, and after a while I was talking to people about organizing a computer club, an adult education course, and various other computer-oriented school activities. I began to hear about more and more operations which could be assisted by computer, and eventually wound up with enough ideas to create a new job in the school.

During the middle months of the year, therefore, most of my spare energies were spent in these preparations, and perhaps partly because of this, I missed the mid-February slump. This had been advertised by my mentors at the university as probably the worst period of the year for everyone. It didn't occur to me that I was supposed to have been depressed until sometime in the spring. Perhaps, also, team teaching kept us all too keyed up to let each other down at this time. This is not to say that we were always bright and cheery. Our morale took a definite drop about two months before the end of the year, in stark contrast to the gradually improving weather. By this time, all of us were veterans who had settled our contracts in one way or another; and had become divided into two camps: those of us who had other plans for next year were coasting along, while the others were busy ordering books and planning courses for the fall. Since there was still the big push of exam week and final grades to be gotten out, we all convinced ourselves that it was time to rest and gather energy for this last effort. The students, at the same time, saw the end in sight and were equally willing to rest on their past laurels. This made them a little less than their usually cooperative selves.

During this critical period, one of the freshman teachers was to give a lecture on industrial growth to my general science large-group session. His plan was to show a filmstrip on the subject, enriching it with his own commentary. Although this technique had been standard practice for the freshmen, it was something unheard of for the juniors, who looked down on the procedure as some sort of a "cop-out" or, at least, as an insult to their intelligence. The situation might not have been so bad if, in addition, he had not encountered difficulty in setting up the filmstrip projector. I believe that these were the worst forty minutes I have ever spent in that room. There we were with 210 sixteen-year olds, as interested in industrial growth as in East-Indian pottery, on a sunny May day in a hot auditorium.

At first I hoped to get the machine figured out and going quickly before the lecture started. But as the minutes dragged on and the fighting junior spirit rose, it became clear that the lecture would have to begin without a working projector in order to "keep the lid on." So I suggested to my partner that he begin while I continued the technical duel. Well, he began, but the juniors did not stop. A dull, widespread mumbling persisted through his introduction. Unfortunately, he chose to ignore it, expecting it to die out. (After many hours in front of that large group, I had learned one thing: dull, widespread mumblings which are ignored do not remain ignorable for long.) I was in a poor position to act upon this wisdom, being without the microphone and being reluctant to leave the intricacies of higher optics. I managed occasional penetrating stares at choice corners of the room. This resulted in temporary lulls (not to mention burnt fingers), and the situation remained ugly until I, armed with pen, paper, and a fighting-mad expression, marched through the room with detentions quite obviously in mind. Five minutes of this hovering threat sufficed to bring the room back to normal, by which time my poor comrade had run out of material and was signaling frantically for the machine. After a brief, but not too humble apology for the infernal contraption, I reminded the masses that there was nothing particularly extraordinary happening before them, and that they would just have to wait patiently until I had the machine repaired. Any undue noise while I was working on it would result in severe handling. This seemed to keep them quiet until I had finished. Now that the machine was working, we faced the next problem: In order to see a filmstrip, it is necessary to extinguish the lights, a move best made only under the most carefully controlled circumstances. With twenty minutes left in the session, there seemed nothing else to do, so we tried it. Occasional noises punctuated the filmstrip (which was, I must admit, pretty dull). Several pitched pennies followed, and I searched my mind for an appropriate action. If I had been able to think of a dozen questions on industrial growth, I would have stopped the whole proceedings instantly and given a quiz. But I couldn't, and I wasn't sure my fellow sufferer could either, or he might have done the same. Finally the time was up and the class came to an uneasy end. The feeling of relief following such a session is intense. I retired to the faculty lounge for the next twenty minutes to brood.

As if to finish up the year with a bang, one of the most embarrassing and infuriating episodes of the year occurred during the last week of school. One of my students, a senior, had not made an appearance in large-group sessions or seminars for about a week. I had assumed that she was just getting "senior-itis" and was willing to sacrifice her grade for the last quarter, since she was not in danger of failing the course, anyway. She had never been a terribly conscientious student, and so I did not notice anything particularly alarming until she was also absent from the final examination. This was something else again. Students who miss final examinations are supposed to be given a mark of incomplete for the year until the exam is made up. But since she was a senior, supposedly graduating in a few days, and since she had not made any arrangements with me for taking the final, I took another look at my grade book for a clue to her behavior. Nasty suspicions started stirring when I remembered that I had never given her a grade for the second quarter of the year. I recalled that she had told me at the time that she was dropping down to the B-track general science course because she had never taken one of the required courses for physics. About six weeks later, she reappeared, saying that she had convinced "the office" that she would have no trouble in the class and that she needed the course for college. Well, she had an honest face, so I never bothered to check into it. But now, with her final and several assignments missing, I suddenly would not have trusted her to tell me the time of day. So I checked with the senior teachers, both of whom knew who she was. They told me that they had never seen her in any of their classes that year. I checked with the office to find out what schedule changes she had made during the year. She had changed to an algebra-trig course, and had dropped family living, but had made no changes in science! Yours truly had let this girl get away with six weeks of vacation in the middle of the year and had *finally* found out about it. My fury could only be compared with that of a jilted woman. I would have had her boiled in oil, if at all possible. However, it was just one day too late in the year. Warnings to seniors who were potential failures were required by law to be sent out the day before, and grades were due shortly. There was very little I could do. I was not able to fail her, thereby delaying her graduation, and I could hardly recover the lost six weeks. At the most, I could rake her over the coals for a little while and hopefully show her that I had not been totally asleep that year. I called her home (getting her mother out of bed, I believe) in an effort to locate her. She was not at home, so I left her mother with the impression that she should report to school at once if she expected to graduate at all. The girl arrived within the hour and told me the same story about prerequisites and attending general science. The senior teachers were standing there listening, and repeated their story. The administrator in charge of schedule changes denied ever having talked to her about prerequisites for physics. Yet she stuck to the story. In my mind, I decided to flunk her for both the second and last quarters and to give her a D in the course, the worst I could do under the circumstances. At this point, however, I wanted her to tell the truth about where she had been during class time, and why, before she graduated from that school. I told her this and added that she would have to take the missing exam the next day, and that, if she had any work which would indicate that she had done a year's work in science, she should bring that along, too. It was all a big bluff, since I was *bound* to pass her, but by then I was learning to bluff. My only further recourse was to visit the superintendent, who suggested that the three of us confer the following day about the matter.

The next morning she took the test. She presented the work that she had failed to bring in during the last few weeks, and finally all but admitted that she had tried to pull a fast one. I expressed surprise that she had thought she could get away with it (shuddering to think that she almost had). I told her that I had not chastised her earlier (LIES! ALL LIES!) because I had been curious to see how much rope she would take to hang herself. I hoped that this story would make her think twice before pulling something similar, even if she might think that she were getting away with it at the time. The lesson, if she learned it at all, was not given too soon. She was off to college about three days after graduation. It would be interesting to hear how she gets through four years of higher education.

The year had, very definitely, a happy ending. The last week of school was one more joyous day after the other, as one computer-scored final after another bit the dust. Although there was plenty of work for all, it was tinged with the knowledge that in a few days we would all be free. The last few days of classes (which were mixed in with finals, for curious reasons) were usually self-evaluative. "What were the best and worst large-groups, labs, seminars of the year?" Many students actually seemed incapable of thinking of the worst ones—"They were all bad" was the most common response, of course. But their faces belied their words. "The best one was when you stepped into the sink of water, Mr. Crawford."

For me, the very best day was the last. All along I had expected pranks near the end, so when our last hour finally came and only one false-alarm (or "student-initiated drill," as we called it) had been pulled, the heat was off. The whole last day was a vacation in itself. It consisted of homeroom, where final announcements were read and good-byes were said. After homeroom, any remaining dirty lockers were cleaned out, and the day was officially over. This left time for the students to roam the halls in search of favorite teachers to sign yearbooks. If ever there was a teacher recognition day, this was it! The same students who usually charged for the doors at 2:59 stayed around, sometimes even waiting in line to receive a few words scrawled by a beaming faculty member. The teachers of the seniors were the busiest, to be sure, but we all got our share of attention. There was little doubt that those who had not signed up to teach next year were regretting it already.

Linda Corman

Hangman or Victim

Apprehensive, but strangely hopeful, I sat in the faculty lounge drinking my fourth cup of coffee for the morning and trying vainly to focus my jittery thoughts on the day ahead. The courses I was to teach should be interesting; the teachers I had met seemed pleasant enough and quite inspired. They were, for the most part, very young; but they seemed altogether confident and in control of their situations. Why, I puzzled, do *I* never feel so secure? Where was I taught to tremble at the prospect of a public test of my talent? After all, I reasoned, this *is* the first day of school—of teaching in a totally unfamiliar setting. But I knew that security and confidence were not simply blessings bestowed on those who reached the second day. My fears were rooted more deeply; they were old friends, not those fleeting,. innocuous acquaintances associated with the unknown—or the soon-to-be-known.

I had never expected to have two "first days" during my first year of teaching. I had supposed that I should have one rather terrifying first day, whose errors and traumas would quickly recede in my memory as subsequent success and growth and pleasure in my work swelled in the foreground of my professional dreams. I had not supposed that I would feel failure and frustration to the exclusion of all but the most inevitable pleasure resulting from those few very special encounters with students or colleagues. I had not expected to give up—to quit my first teaching job at mid-year and change to a new school, where I would have to survive another "first day," another test.

Again I was hopeful, but on this second "first day" I could not keep from remembering the past five months, from wondering if things would really be different, or if I would have to endure it all again. It *had* been horrible, I thought; it wasn't my imagination. At times during the last few weeks, after having decided to leave, I had doubted the necessity, the wisdom of my decision. Things were going pretty well; I was becoming involved with many of my students in a positive way and enjoying considerable success teaching *The Old Man and the Sea*. Perhaps I had been too hasty; perhaps it just takes time. But probably, I thought, my life in this school is more bearable only because I know that soon I will leave. And it had, after all, been horrible. I was bewildered by having lived through it and even more bewildered by trying to figure out exactly what it was that I had lived through, *when* I had given up, and *why*. A poem came to mind—a speech by the Marquis de Sade in Peter Weiss's play. I had never completely understood these words when I first read them as a student. Unlike most of his words in the play, these seemed exclusively applicable to his own perverted temperament. Or so I then thought. I suppose it all started when I was still a student.

> Before deciding what is wrong and what is right
> first we must find out what we are
> I do not know myself
> No sooner have I discovered something
> than I begin to doubt it
> and I have to destroy it again
> What we do is just a shadow of what we want to do
> and the only truths we can point to
> are the ever-changing truths of our own experience
> I do not know if I am hangman or victim
> for I imagine the most horrible tortures
> and as I describe them I suffer them myself
> There is nothing that I could not do and everything
>   fills me with horror
> And I see that other people also
> suddenly change themselves into strangers
> and are driven to unpredictable acts

Considering myself sophisticated enough to survive any experience the outside world was pleased to offer, I lent a deaf ear and bored spirit to academic discussions of the severe "cultural shocks" we, who then dwelt in University of Chicago ivory-towerdom, were likely to undergo on the job. I had attended the only public high school in my small midwestern hometown and had therefore been exposed, I thought, to the social, emotional, and intellectual lives of a socioeconomic cross section of teenagers and to the academic dispositions of variously talented young students. I had also known urban youth, black and white, in college and before. I had known and liked very well the blacks with whom I became acquainted in college. Certainly, I asserted, I was altogether sympathetic with the plight of minority groups and totally without so-called prejudice. And I had traveled a lot on my own and, after all, had lived in Chicago's liberal melting pot, Hyde Park, for a year. On the whole, I concluded, I had met a varied lot of people and should no doubt find very little new—certainly nothing surprising—in anyone whom I should hereafter encounter.

Perhaps I had simply forgotten these people of my past. For, it turned out that I was thoroughly shocked by a large portion of the high school community with which I sought to involve myself. Only now can I see that these people should have been familiar from the beginning. I had read about them in books—in novels and poems, in psychology texts and anthropological studies. And most of them I had indeed known very well before.

But I did not know myself, and I did not know the role I haphazardly tried to play. I had known tyrant-teachers and pushovers, bright ones and ignorant ones; but I had not known them as colleagues. I had known mischievous students and helpful ones, vicious ones and apple-polishers, but I had not known them as students in a class I was supposed to teach. I had known principals and assistant principals, and counselors and truant officers, but I had not known them as one who expected to be treated as the college graduate, the lady, and the professional I wanted desperately to be. In short, I saw strange faces because I looked out through the strangely new eyes of a teacher.

The first unsettling relationship I experienced was between myself-as-bookkeeper and the assistant principal, who was chief disciplinarian for teachers as well as for students. At that point I assumed that our relationship was a unique one, that the small but fierce-looking gentleman, whom I faintly recognized from somewhere in *David Copperfield*, particularly relished *my* suffering and soon would instruct the lunchroom ladies that my daily fare should not exceed two chunks of bread and a cup of lukewarm water—that is, until I had successfully distributed the hundreds of computer-information forms apparently required for the official organization of my thirty-five-student homeroom. To complete these forms, the teacher must obtain endless numbers of names, telephone numbers, fathers' birthplaces—all of which were forthcoming only by means of illegal lashings or calls to guardians whose telephone numbers one is seeking!

Playing private secretary to thirty-five students was an exasperating but eye-opening experience. For who would have guessed that blanks requiring a guardian's name or a home address might constitute for some young people a legitimately difficult, perhaps impossible task? One boy had moved around from aunt to friend for the past two years, never quite sure where he would be wanted or want to stay. A girl didn't really know if the cousin with whom she had lived since her mother's disappearance a year ago was her guardian or not. And I had never known anyone who refused to reveal his phone number because his mother's welfare payments would be jeopardized if knowledge of her having a telephone fell into the wrong hands. But I did not have time to digest these strange new things, for unfilled blanks kept flowing in. The censure I received for my shortcomings in this role of private secretary was the final humiliation—and a useless one at that, for indeed, I was trying very hard.

This completely unexpected burden occupied more time than class preparations, or rather usurped the time allotted for class preparations during the first few weeks of school and frequently thereafter. And the assistant principal was the living symbol of this burden to me, since it was usually he who stalked furiously in and out during class or homeroom periods to chastise me for my errors and delays in fulfilling my clerical duties. He also made a practice of sending for me while I was teaching, requesting that I come immediately to his office, where he would point out a mistake I had made in signing a readmission blank. By the time I returned to my class, the always tenuous state of readiness for learning had wholly dissolved into a chaos that I could not hope, at least that day, to subdue. Later I discovered that all teachers were treated precisely the same way—and all parents and students as well! I was not being singled out and I was not particularly inefficient. But in the beginning I did not know this and was not confident enough to oppose the assistant principal as, I learned later, everyone, to some extent, must do. Simply to refuse to come to his office had never occurred to me. I felt that I was a persecuted failure.

For several weeks I attributed virtually all my disappointments, fears, and failures to this man; he became, in effect, the scapegoat whom I regularly sacrificed in the purgation rituals of my nocturnal fantasies. He preserved himself quite vigorously in those nightmares, however, playing the torturer at least as frequently as the victim. The former role suited him with uncanny perfection, given that he was an altogether terrifying disciplinarian, at whose threats I had often seen young offenders tremble. Furthermore, he had tufts of red hair sticking straight up on each side of his head, giving the unmistakable illusion of satanic horns!

The irrationality which abounds in the preceding discussion will not, I hope, be condemned, but rather recognized as the unfortunate state into which my customary sanity and sensibility had descended during the first weeks of my first teaching experience. However humorous or ridiculous it may seem now, it was thoroughly debilitating and horrifying at the time. A backward glance today, however, reveals this state of mind to be far healthier than that to which it gave birth. For in the beginning I opposed myself essentially to a system—a system which left me neither the time nor the energy to care much about my students, and which harassed me with petty mistakes. As I gradually adjusted to the bureaucracy of the system, a second, more significant conflict emerged.

The philosophy of "discipline" and the apparent relationship between teacher and student at my school mushroomed suddenly to loom over my new professional life in stark contrast to my own ideals. The best teacher was the toughest—that is, the man who flunked the largest percentage of his students and spent half his class time clearing out the halls and organizing the up and down staircases; the woman who shouted "shut up" louder than the rest and justified her humiliating punishment of a student simply with, "Because I don't like your face." The insults flung at students were offensive; those received by teachers I was yet to know.

I felt only contempt at that point for the offending teachers and rejected the system which engendered and glorified them, a system which rendered ineffectual the basically idealistic, humanistic principal assigned to the school. Where was that respect for the student I had learned to expect from teachers? I sensed only hostility and hatred, distrust and condescension. But worst of all, as I was to learn well, there was *fear*—latent perhaps, but underlying everything.

Within a period of three or four years, the ethnic population of the school had changed drastically. The number of honors classes had been cut sharply, and the classes in lower tracks increased. Teachers felt compelled to lower their standards in order to pass a sufficient number of students. (The principal was displeased— and legitimately so, for reasons many teachers refused to see— with a failure rate of more than 12 percent.) But most important, teachers were faced with the challenge of completely revising their methods in order to remain effective with the new crop of students.

The established faculty core was threatened from all sides— from new teachers, from the unpopular "liberal" principal, and from the new students and their families. They were not familiar with the methods and materials required by the changing population, and they were not particularly interested anyway. They avoided the establishment of unified faculty goals and curriculum plans which required communication and intra-faculty criticism. Socially they were friends; they played bridge together in the lounge. But when it came to the job, each teacher preferred to close his door to the rest of the world and exercise unlimited and uncriticized authority in his own classroom. So little communication existed between members of the English department, for example, that I discovered one particular literature textbook used by all teachers of all four grades and two different tracks. A student could conceivably read the same collection of appropriate but literarily insignificant stories in each of his four high school years of English. And furthermore, it is most likely that the teachers would all use the convenient teaching edition of this text, thus exposing this hypothetical student to precisely the same questions about the stories in all four years, to the same background information, and to the same introductory gimmick designed to entice him to read! Highly structured and narrowly defined curricula are frequently dreaded and denounced by students in education, and by teachers themselves. And for good reason: *Great Expectations* might well be one teacher's triumph and another's nightmare. And a narrowly defined goal, particularly in English, is frighteningly liable to be wrong. But without a sense of functioning within and for the sake of a larger whole, the individual teacher (perhaps especially the new one, for whom self-evaluation and realistic goal-setting are difficult) labors under a frequently intolerable belief in the futility and insignificance of his minute role in a student's life. The freedom which teaching in such a department affords is considerably clouded by the inefficiency it ordinarily nourishes.

Insecurity pervaded the atmosphere of this school, infecting student, teacher, and administrator. Having been, if anything, over-secure about my own strength, I had developed no immunity to this particular infection. I could not bear it—or ignore it.

As I began to recognize the shells into which many of the more established teachers withdrew, in their professional roles, I also began to understand why this happened. They were afraid of the new student body, which few of them were prepared to educate. The professional challenge—or threat—posed by these young people was met, as a rule, by one of two attitudes: either savage scorn for students, with explicit denunciation of them emotionally and intellectually, or feigned sympathy, apparent indulgence, and finally, pity. Both of these student-teacher relationships precluded the mutual respect which I believe the process of education, particularly in the arts, requires. Nor were these relationships satisfying to the teacher; he knew he was failing, either refusing or unable to meet the challenge of the "new" school. For the most part he would not admit it, living instead in constant fear that his colleagues would discover him.

This, of course, I did not understand at all in the beginning. The apparent hostility and isolationism of teachers was totally incomprehensible and disturbing to me. Asking a colleague about his classroom activities was usually interpreted as something very suspicious and was either rudely rebuffed or glibly avoided. All in all I felt very much alone and professionally insecure. Undoubtedly I would do everything wrong. Since I had very little idea what ninth grade regular classes in this high school ought to be doing, as opposed to tenth or eleventh grade honors classes, or to classes in a suburban high school, the odds were convincingly in favor of my doing the wrong thing. Or so I thought. But I had to do *something*. And it really didn't matter much anyway, so long as nobody noticed, I thought. As long as I kept my door and my mouth shut as much as possible and polished up a set of "good" answers for any official questions likely to be asked. Suddenly I had arrived—another silent, mysterious member of the English faculty. At that point I was even unable to choose a master teacher to be officially my friend, or something of that sort. Of course, I was yet new; later when a small clique of the faculty convened at a local tavern after open house, I did meet those in my department who might have made all the difference to me in the beginning. But they appeared too late. Perhaps if there had been a departmental meeting—

However deeply I had fallen into the pattern of faculty membership that I witnessed around me, I never acquired the discretion sufficient to carry it off. By confessing that I had assigned no grammar text to my classes and, in fact, would probably not even teach grammar on its own, I managed to let myself in for a most unfriendly assault directed primarily, it seemed, at my youthful arrogance. Furthermore, it was the sin of my counterparts who managed to infiltrate the grammar schools that freshmen came to high school so completely illiterate these days! Though I suffered intensely, there were no repercussions from this incident, for as I said, the teachers' philosophy was strictly laissez-faire.

My assailant in the above incident ordinarily displayed a rather merry, earthy temper, shouting invectives vigorously at boys scuffling outside the lunchroom door, while amusing his table companions with gay tales of his youth and colorfully frank condemnations of school policy and policymakers. He wasn't very popular with students, as far as I could tell; this concerned me because I was sure he cared sincerely for them, in spite of his stern ways, which is a great deal more than one could say for most of the more popular teachers. In any event, I was violently shocked to hear one morning that students had entered the school building the previous night with stolen keys to deposit human excrement on this particular teacher's desk. Because his room doubled as the faculty lunchroom, however, the precise target of this unusual prank was never absolutely clear.

When the term's activities had settled down into somewhat of a routine, teachers began to be absent frequently. During two of my extra-duty periods, I was regularly assigned to cover classes for the absent teachers. (Substitutes were luxurious commodities at this school.) At first, my one guaranteed "guidance" period was often also taken up with other classes. On some days I was in class eight periods a day. Since discipline is much more exhausting if there is little or no teaching involved and if the teacher is a substitute, the added burden of covering two or three extra classes (two of which came before my own classes began for the day) sapped a great deal of the spirit I originally enjoyed in my own classes.

When the last thirty-six fifteen-year-olds of the day plunked their restless, bored faces in front of me, I was neither inspired nor especially interested, but simply exhausted and nervously suspicious. Every natural, end-of-the-day expression from the students became a personal threat to my authority. I quickly developed paranoia toward this class, and they toward me. The pursuit of authority for its own sake began gradually to consume my goals and dissipate my emotional energy. More and more I needed to be obeyed. And this situation arose, I think, largely out of my difficulties with the extra classes I was required to cover, when the object was simply to *control* the class, a task infinitely more difficult when a teacher has strange students and unfamiliar material. When I began regularly to face two classes primed for a substitute, before entering my own, my morale rapidly sunk and my rational faculty succumbed in an emotional upheaval which I failed entirely to survive.

Perhaps the final straw was an incident which occurred when I was covering an upper-grade social studies class on an otherwise hectic day. I entered the class with the defensive sneer I had for some reason elected to copy from those tyrant-teachers I once despised. In the coldest tone possible I instructed the class to remain perfectly silent, with at least the appearance of serious intent, for the rest of the forty minutes. At this point a mocking female voice blared out with sarcastic laughter. A boy said he had to see the janitor and walked out before I could stop him. But the girl, I thought, would suffer. I told her to keep her stupid mouth shut and copy word-for-word a chapter from her history textbook. She laughed again, at which point a worldly-looking black girl behind her smiled coolly and said to me: "Niggers are nasty, aren't they? You don't like niggers, do you?" And to her friend she said, "She doesn't like you, black girl, can't you see?" I don't remember what I thought or what happened for the next few minutes, except I could see only this girl and hear only her sneering insults. And I prayed that she wouldn't say anything else, because I didn't know what to do. When the attendance list came to her she signed a phony name, so I asked her what her name was. She wanted to know why I asked, and I told her that her regular teacher would no doubt be interested in hearing what she had had to say in class while he was gone. She laughed, "Don't worry, he's black too."

Nothing remotely similar to this had ever happened to me, in my own classes or any time in my life. But I wonder now if it was really because the people were different or because I was different, bossing them around as if they were convicts, and perhaps hating them for—I thought—making me do it. In any case, when I could take it no longer and realized something had to be done, I took the girl to the disciplinarian, a step that I had never previously taken. In the end this girl and the one who had laughed were expelled for a few days. Unfortunately the incident was not over for me. The worldly one of the two turned out to be notorious for her rude pseudosophisticated conduct, her dubious income, and her enormous influence in the Black Power group at the school. From that day forward, even my own classes never seemed the same again. I saw the girl from time to time in the corridor talking to my students, and afterwards I sensed their hostility and felt that they were quietly conspiring against me. I was thoroughly terrified. Perhaps it was all my imagination; undoubtedly it was partially this. But it didn't matter in practice. No rationalization could alleviate the nausea I felt every morning before school. No rationalization could restore the mutual trust and friendship which had characterized my relationships with most of my students previously. I felt continually threatened by the sullen, more sophisticated black girls in my classes. I dreamed about them at night and tried to avoid catching their eyes in the daytime. It was unbearable. I dreaded having that same girl in a class I would be asked to cover in the future.

And things got worse. I approached my own classes with fear masked in tyranny and quickly lost rapport, then control. I had to leave. What had begun as an inconvenience had become a personal disaster. Compelled by the system to do inhuman jobs, I was victimized by it, as the others had been. I had come to evaluate myself by their standards, standards I had rejected totally four months earlier. I tried unsuccessfully to adopt their methods. A good class was a quiet class; therefore, I was a failure. I still despised them, but now I was one of them. Craving dignity, elegance, and beauty, I had become base and vulgar and thus could see only the base and vulgar wherever I looked. Dedicated to teaching literature and language as the means to experience and express the highest values of human life, I had become less than human, utterly incapable of success, on my old terms as well as the new ones. I wanted to start over. And I *had* to leave.

My second "first day" as a teacher began in an unusual school. The new school was an alternative to the public school system, a second chance school. The student body would not be made up of honor society aspirants, cheerleaders, and athletic stars. Instead there would be students hardened by their failures in other schools and the failures of other teachers to win their interest in school subjects.

Predictably, the events of this fearfully anticipated second "first day" were anticlimactic: The most formidable challenge was trying to consume a respectable portion of the ninety-minute periods, after five months of racing through fleeting forty-minute periods. And the only major "trauma" suffered was overhearing an attractive, popular female member of my new English literature class chuckle to a friend about "the terrified new teacher," who seemed to expect the class to use switchblades to protest her reading list. Indeed, it had been somewhat unnerving to stand before sixteen- to twenty-five year olds, including Vietnam veterans, gang members, and hippie "acid-heads," rather than the fourteen-year-olds I then fondly remembered as gentle innocents! Certainly it seemed a bit odd to see students smoking in the corridors during breaks. But for a school designed to meet the special needs (and often whims) of young people who, for one reason or another, hadn't made it in public school, the place seemed remarkably stable and at ease—comfortable, in fact. There would be times of disorder and conflict, but only under extraordinary circumstances: the day after the death of Dr. King and the last day of classes. On the whole, however, my impressions on this first day proved valid. Underneath a surface of permissiveness and apparent disorder lay a generally effective educational structure, strengthened by the freedom and independence enjoyed by the students, and the responsibilities borne by them.

Minimal bureaucratic busy-work, a realistic teaching load (three ninety-minute classes a day), and sophisticated students combined to alleviate the anxiety with which I had abandoned my previous teaching position, realizing that if the change brought no improvement, I should have to look outside the field altogether for my niche. I had expected from the beginning to encounter endless problems in secondary school teaching. But I expected these problems to be a kind that I could define and attack—such as unsuccessful material or methods, curriculum inadequacies, individual students needing help of one kind or another from me. And at last these problems—these attackable problems—began to emerge from the vague despair which had instead enveloped my premiere in the profession.

Although I had previously taught a charmingly outspoken young ninth-grader, who daily suggested improvements in my teaching methods, the aggressively critical students with whom I now dealt were a total surprise. The last thing I expected from public school rejects out to get a quick, if expensive, diploma was serious, perceptive criticism of exactly what they were expected to learn. And I responded with characteristically ruffled feathers at first, haughtily defending my reading lists and class activities. Then one day, when I asked a student in class to tell me about the problems of Holden Caulfield, he flatly refused, asserting: "I don't care about the problems of Holden Caulfield; I don't care why he hated nose-picking, and I don't care what the nuns had to do with the prostitute, or with anybody else." I couldn't bring myself to ask him what he *did* care about—not during class. For I knew that he was right, and even that I would care more about that too; and I was afraid that everyone would think I didn't really care at all about them—for they had all been telling me for the longest time the same thing. Nevertheless, I had plugged away, with new tricks and fancy games, sure that they would one day love this novel. But I hadn't really thought about *why* they should love it, or what it would really mean to *them,* or if there were not something they might profit more from reading, and understand better. In short, I had not thought about them as individual, thinking, feeling human beings, artificially forced into a classroom, whose artificiality was heightened by a teacher who hadn't yet managed to find time for the individual student, *qua* man. After class I asked the student what he *did* care about, why he had lately been so lazy and quiet in class? And he told me that his mother had died last week (he had no father) and that he had just had a little son (he wasn't married) and that his brother was missing in action in Vietnam.

After trying without success to play a teacher-as-authority role for five months, I realized at last that I could and must accept students on a more or less equal basis, respecting their criticism and their judgment in the classroom, as well as in the halls. But I went further than that. I plunged blindly off my theoretical pedestal into the emotional gutters of education's thoroughfares. That is, I began to try exclusively to *please*. In effect, I begged, offered "candy," or performed, trying almost everything short of jumping out of a cake and doing a striptease dance on the desk (which, with my students, would have been good for only one show, in any event!)—*anything* to amuse and please them, or, if you will, "to turn the kids on."

One of the virtues of this school was that its faculty unanimously considered themselves responsible for sincerely motivating the never-before-motivated young people who end up there. But fundamental disagreements would certainly have destroyed faculty unanimity on this subject if a common goal of motivation were to be sought. To *what,* exactly, were we "turning the kids on"? They were given enormous freedom: no study periods or required activities outside of academic classes, which were finished at 1:00 P.M. every day; permission to smoke anywhere except in the classrooms; the opportunity to receive credit for supervised independent study. Students who broke rules (or public laws) were given chance after chance to shape up. The individual human value and dignity of every student was officially recognized and respected; he in turn was expected to prove the school was right in trusting and respecting him. This independence enjoyed by students precluded entirely that tyrant-mystique with which teachers ("masters") have traditionally subdued students. In order to survive here, a teacher had to do more than simply stand scowling in front of a class: to a significant extent he had to *please* his students.

On another level educators have been attempting to please students by giving them new positions of significant power in the school structure. Movements for increased student power are widespread in the United States today, and our school was no exception. The administration suggested at one point that the newly formed student council, which had evolved more or less into a Black Power group, have jurisdiction over certain difficult discipline cases, including the mugging of a white student by a black student, and several cases of extortion. The students shunned this responsibility, asserting that discipline was an administrative function. They agreed to cooperate by advising on occasion, but most students felt it was unfair to them and dangerous to their loyalties and friendships to burden them with this authority.

It was also suggested that students be given power in hiring and firing faculty members. That such moves are being seriously considered indicates for one thing the seriousness of the "turn the kids on" trend in education. The faculty again became passionately divided into factions corresponding roughly with the results of an informal popularity poll conducted by students to rate their teachers. Teachers opposing the grant of such power to the students claimed that when a teacher knows such a judgment will be made by students, it becomes even harder to think about teaching rather than merely pleasing the students. A teacher then becomes more of a politician than a statesman. Many teachers were of the opinion that under such conditions they would feel compelled to be more permissive than they thought healthful.

However, the permissiveness of our school was continually defended by students and faculty alike in an attempt, probably, to rationalize the atmosphere of the school, which to an outsider must certainly have appeared somewhat less than conducive to learning. To be sure, class discussions were stimulating, uninhibited, and in many ways shockingly enlightening to a degree unimaginable in most public school classrooms. By the same token they could be terrifying and destructive at times, to a degree more blatant, if not more absolute, than one would experience in an average public school classroom. But in spite of the unique problems that arose in this school and the singular adjustments that had to be made there, certain conflicts emerged which, in the final analysis, are probably universal to the first-year teaching experience, wherever or with whomever it occurs.

Because our students had proved their need for extraordinary "inspiration," we felt justified in worrying perhaps more than usual about that thing which is now called "turning the kids on" and which corresponds, I suppose, to the old "motivation" worries. How much time can and should be devoted to winning over those stoic, hostile, or distracted minds in an English literature class? Should one start right out with *Hamlet* or *Beowulf,* or would a couple of days be well spent on lyrics to the Beatles' songs—even though there are only nine weeks to cover fifteen centuries of that glorious corpus of beauty and truth to the promulgation of which I often assumed that I had dedicated my life? Given this conflict, which I think most teachers feel, many problems arise—between student and teacher and among faculty members themselves.

I declare at the outset that, though a teacher, I am altogether human: I want to be accepted, to be liked, to succeed, to feel strength or, perhaps, power. One way to do this—the quickest way, I found—is to appeal directly to the students. This doesn't necessarily mean turning one's classroom into a carnival, but it does mean seeking and taking seriously student feedback. A teacher who plays the role, consciously or otherwise, of an overgrown adolescent, a "with-it" hippie, or the like, often enjoys quite a headstart on the academic, theory-befuddled graduate. Once when I was playing a Donovan recording of Shakespeare's lyric "Under the Greenwood Tree," a student observed: "When we listened to this record in Mr. Krick's class, we turned the lights out and he let us smoke so we could really groove it; this is a drag." Thinking that I had been quite clever and appealing in bringing a popular folk ballad to my English literature class, my hopes fell painfully at this remark and I turned my disappointment into resentment against the other teacher, who had broken school regulations, I felt, at my expense, making my job even more difficult. Such feelings, I soon realized, were not unusual among teachers. In fact, they were so widespread that in the end the faculty literally blew up. Under the guise of quibbling over abuse of a rule about field trips, faculty hostilities were vented with gusto. And these hostilities proceeded from experiences very much like the one I have recalled above. Naturally the "bread and circuses" teachers were those who constantly took their students out of classes to attend movies, to visit art galleries, and for similar intrinsically worthwhile activities—usually without providing sufficient advance warning to other teachers, from whose classes students were to be excused. As a result—or rather as the culmination of accumulated hostilities—the faculty divided into cutthroat factions, ostensibly over this particular practice. This faculty division, tied up with an abortive attempt to unionize, generated a professional tension which, for a time, greatly diminished, if not entirely dissipated, my energy for classroom activity.

For the first time I realized the naïveté with which I had blamed many of the problems of my first school on the total lack of formal faculty communication, or regular faculty meetings. Ironically, faculty meetings and the drawn out, destructive failures of communication they promoted became for awhile a major source of disillusionment and discontent for me at this second school. It became all too clear that secondary education was not simply university life on a lower level; I again longed (probably naïvely) for the rationality of the ivory tower, for the companionship of human beings who could somehow divorce intellectual or professional activities from their own personal neuroses and fetishes. But the extent to which I too began to indulge in public displays of irrationality and insecurity, in shouting battles and emotion-laden attacks, bothered me most of all. Nor did it end at the school door. The "truth sessions" into which the administration had proudly maneuvered the faculty meetings left their mark on my personal life as well, causing me for a while to approach every conversation defensively or offensively, loudly and childishly.

But to bring this whole conflict to a personal level, its most acute manifestation was in the issue of teaching and/or pleasing young people. I wanted very much to be liked by the students; I probably wanted their affection and acceptance more than I wanted their intellectual growth during most of this first year. I was jealous of teachers whose classes received enthusiastic approval from students who were telling me what was wrong with mine. Though I constantly requested suggestions from students and encouraged their comments on my classes and their freedom of speech and opinion, I must have secretly desired only praise, for I was always quite thoroughly depressed by criticism, and at first inwardly reacted only with defense. And of all criticism, the kind I found most unbearably painful was that which hinged on an unfavorable comparison of my class to another teacher's.

Perhaps the lesson hardest to learn during the first year of teaching was that I could not be the same kind of teacher as someone else. Although I had watched expert seamstresses and golfers and profited from imitating their actions and methods, I could not seem to gain from imitating those whom I thought successful teachers. Teaching, I finally decided, is somehow too closely knit into the basic fabric of one's character and personality to be copied. Just as I cannot take the place of a father for my students, for obvious reasons, so also I cannot be a successful radical in the classroom, when as a person I am, generally speaking, conservative. My efforts to align myself with ultra-liberals (who tend usually to gain the sympathy and rapport of youth) were on the whole "discovered" and in some fashion denounced as fake. The dangers incurred in assuming a persona too far from the "real" me became most glaringly ominous along a slightly different line. When I tried to become "one of the crowd," I could only be assimilated in terms meaningful to the crowd and realistically applicable to me; the only aspects of "me" which truly fit into the crowd were of course those totally unrelated to my role as teacher. I was accepted as a young, somewhat inconsistent female, who appeared to be trying very hard to please, a posture all too frequently interpreted as flirting.

Henry, for example, who was twenty-one years old, rarely worked efficiently in composition class, but when he worked, he showed considerable ability. I found that warmly asking him to write something for me was an effective motivational technique. It was too late when I discovered that it motivated more than interesting essays. Henry became loud and offensive in class, and began to come to class high on something. I learned the hard way that once a personal relationship is established (via smiles, feminine cajolery, or whatever, rather than constructive advice and professional assistance), *all* interaction will be taken personally, including negative criticism and humiliating disciplinary gestures. Without realizing it, I had become for Henry a woman with whom he had a very personal relationship; I teased him and wheedled him into working, and he worked to please me. When I appeared to reject or insult him, I reinforced all the rejections and insults he had endured from women throughout his life, and he reacted as he always had: he rebelled, tried to shock me, and ran away from it all by drinking or smoking marijuana before class. At least this is the way I finally understood the situation from subsequent discussions with Henry. Understanding it, however, never really healed any wounds. It was a mistake which, like most I made in my first year of teaching, can never be quite expiated, much less undone. Such mistakes can be shoved into the background and overcome, but I remain haunted by the realization that each student's life is successfully or unsuccessfully related to mine; each student constitutes for me a victory or a defeat, with a kind of finality, a conclusion. Helping one young person does not cancel out hurting another.

Henry was not the only student who suffered because of my role-playing complications. Besides young men in comparable situations, there were also the other women in the classroom. I look back now on my confrontation at the first school with the antagonistic young woman who so violently influenced those weeks. At work in that situation were probably much the same forces that I later met head on. If young male students are confused about the woman-teacher's role in their lives, so also their girl-friends are confused by this role.

I had had a particularly friendly and mature young man in class for two consecutive quarters, during both of which I enjoyed his contributions in the classroom and his conversation outside of class. Clark, as a rule, received B's in my classes. Throughout the second quarter I seemed constantly to be involved in minor discipline clashes with the young lady who was seated next to Clark. Nothing seemed to work with this student, and I finally became resigned to the situation and ignored her barely audible insults in class and her rude behavior toward me in the halls. When one day she received (with loudly vocalized astonishment!) a grade of B, when Clark had received only a C, the fog lifted and I saw that for a long time she had looked on me as a contemporary competing for the interest of Clark and rewarding (or seducing) him with higher grades. Once again, however, understanding brought much less than a quick and adequate solution. "Cooling it" with Clark was a rather delicate enterprise, for I feared consequences comparable to those in the case of Henry. The year ended just in time, with no final stability realized, but another lesson learned—or *survived* with that bumbling, adrenalin-powered determination so regularly required during this first year.

Most of us have spent some portion of our lives feigning naïveté for one reason or another. And this is the role that I found
most effective during the last weeks of the year. After running
through various personae (in one class I had desperately resorted
to convincing the students I was a Russian princess in exile, which
served my purposes for a week or so!), I finally, for the last
quarter, became the country-born innocent. For example, when
two twenty-four-year-old Vietnam veterans were disturbing the
class by talking in the back row, I simply acted wholeheartedly
surprised and speechless that they would do such a shocking
thing. Boys began apologizing after class for doing things which
had apparently shocked me—things they (and I) had done for
years with hardly a second thought. But it was difficult to keep
from giggling during all this, and I fear it wouldn't have worked
so well much longer. Still, I think it was harmless, useful, amusing, and a good example of the way roles can work for a teacher
who consciously manipulates them in the classroom.

The question of a teacher's role, chosen consciously, or otherwise assumed, implies of course that the teacher has in mind a
certain image to be projected to a class for specific purposes,
to reach conscious goals or satisfy subconscious needs. Many
students throughout the year informed me of my weaknesses,
the greatest of which, according to them, was weakness itself:
"You're too soft." "You oughtta flunk that guy." "The kids will
walk all over you." "You gotta be tougher—stricter—meaner—
you're too nice." "They'll respect you for it in the end."

"They'll respect you for it." Undoubtedly students have no respect for a teacher whom they can consistently demoralize and
deceive. But neither do they respect in a productive way a teacher
whom they fear, mentally as well as physically. And in any case,
I saw immediately that I had little hope for accomplishing my
goals through intimidation. What exactly is the necessary and
sufficient degree of firmness? Precisely how long should the rope
be? These are the questions I constantly faced during the first
year of teaching, and the questions I probably will never finally
answer. Nor, I believe, will anyone be able to answer these questions empirically, for the answers seem necessarily to change,
from teacher to teacher, student to student, day to day, class to
class. Inconsistent, perhaps, but truly human!

Students, I felt, understood and demanded fairness and justice more than anything else in their relationship with me as a teacher. But unfortunately these are concepts impossible for me to define precisely outside of the specific situation. And when one's tolerance, one's state of mind change so radically from class to class, from day to day, where does justice lie? Would it be best, I wondered, to establish rigid but altogether clear and specifiable rules for classroom behavior, at the risk of stultifying discussion and disastrously hampering creative spontaneity? If not, then how does the reticent boy who enjoyed talking in a small group yesterday exactly understand the justice of the reprimand he incurs today for talking to his neighbors? And yet today I had decided that it was crucial for me to lecture for a few minutes to the whole class, to clear up some important points. Can I allow one student to subvert the learning efforts of thirty-four others, and frustrate my carefully constructed plans? Dilemmas such as this made this first year of teaching the challenge that it consistently was—the constantly new, human experience.

Each day took a shape of its own, sometimes as a result of, but usually in spite of, my direction; each day's learning experience was in some respect unique. And I know now that each day's learning *opportunities* are unique and must be uniquely utilized. To illustrate this, I must describe what was probably my greatest success along this line. We were spending a few days on war poetry in one class, and I had duplicated a selection of modern poems dealing with Vietnam, including some from Robert Bly's *The Light Around the Body*. A day or two before we were scheduled to study these, Bly accepted the National Book Award for this volume with a courageous speech urging young men to resist the draft. The speech was colorfully reported in the newspaper most popular with our students and was widely read during first-period classes. In my "Problems and Protest" class that day, a consistently skeptical, science-oriented student suggested that poets never face reality, but rather hide themselves away to write foolish romantic poetry; that poetry in any event is irrelevant to our life; that poets are social parasites; and that we really ought to spend our time discussing important things, such as the war in Vietnam, and get out of this poetry bag. Of course the ending is obvious: We jumped ahead to Bly's poems, discussed them in relation to his speech at the National Book Award ceremony, and established to the satisfaction of one and all the relevance of poetry! It is unlikely that I could have planned a lesson half this successfully, however seriously I had tried or however long I had worked. A day so uniquely perfect for such a lesson could not have been planned—an outside event, a spontaneous student remark, the appropriate body of material at hand, *success!*

Having a student body with backgrounds as diverse as ours, where even common geographical locations did not provide workable generalizations about the students, since they came from all over the city and its suburbs, it was extremely difficult to know exactly where to stand, in order to promote the most effective intellectual and moral growth for *all* the students. Half black and half white, from middle, high-middle, and low income families, from the inner city and the suburb, our students worked together and relaxed together with remarkable equanimity. But in the classroom, walls and pitfalls often developed. Racial attitudes, otherwise obscured, appeared glaringly in a discussion of Baldwin's *Notes of a Native Son.* How much instigating should I do? How much could I responsibly do? Should I allow the complacent middle-class blacks to suffer the attacks of the militants, who called them Toms? Could I afford to alienate the militants by defending the individual black's right to choose the values for his own life, or by reminding them that their arguments resembled those used for decades by whites against blacks? (They thought segregated housing in a university should be allowed because whites steal from them and might attack them in their sleep.) Could I in good conscience encourage my students to demonstrate, to engage in active protests, when they might well get beaten by a policeman in the process of doing this? After all, do I not personally feel that one's own particular life constitutes matter of infinite potential, and that one should not passionately or carelessly sacrifice it without making the most of it first?

The question of "rabble-rousing" in the classroom was of more than merely personal significance. Some teachers solicited the aid of others in actively inciting our students to participate in demonstrations and protests. Other teachers objected to this use of the classroom as a political podium.

The most difficult thing for me throughout this trying time was deciding on the point beyond which I was unqualified to go. Talking of action and "semi-violence" to my college friends was one thing: I could predict their responses; I could count on their responsible consideration of any advice I offered. But I often felt unequipped to cope adequately with the responses of my students to even the simplest classroom stimuli, much less high-powered stimuli concerned with already explosive social situations. Of course I couldn't really *figure out* the right thing to do. Anything I decided could be easily rationalized according to one perfectly valid set of criteria or another. The decision seemed somehow apart from the realm of reason and lodged rather in that of personal honesty—being true to oneself, or something like that.

Why in the first place am I in the teaching field? Why was I an English major? Why do I believe that great books are worth reading? Strangely enough, these questions led me to the answer which worked most efficiently to resolve my conflicts—or at least which led to the most comfortable rationalization, the one truer to myself. I loved literature and philosophy and great books with their great thoughts because they helped me see a superstructure in terms of which this present life, however ugly, seemed worth preserving. They gave me respect for transcendent qualities of human nature, for virtue and beauty and the desire for truth. And I still think these things are important, even after this first remarkable year of teaching! I think that one should examine one's own life not only in terms of the here and now, but in terms of the good, the true, and the beautiful which exist always. I believe that it is human to live partially in a dream, to look beyond the ugliness which may confront one today to a beauty of yesterday or tomorrow, which may never have existed really or will never exist in the future, but which in a present dream glorifies one's human mind. I am prepared to be accused of escapism— even irresponsible escapism! But I decided to teach because I wanted to share with others a view of something beyond the physical, temporal chains by which we are bound; a view of a comforting, exhilarating world of the not-concrete. Truly a student profits only from what he can successfully relate to his own life; but in order to profit, he must be carried beyond what is simply his life as it stands; he must encounter in the classroom, and in great books, those human realms he may enter, which in his "real" life he would never have known.

I remember the moment I became reunited with this, my

original goal. We were discussing in class the assassination of Senator Robert Kennedy, when a student asserted that beyond all doubt the assassin was hired by Senator McCarthy in order to facilitate his presidential campaign. This led to an observation by another student that President John F. Kennedy had been assassinated by hirelings of either Vice-President Johnson or Mrs. Jacqueline Kennedy. At this moment I saw clearly that one must go beyond—far beyond—the spectrum of human experience familiar to many of our youth in order to educate them responsibly to be truly human beings. Rabble-rousing will not do; turning them on is not enough. Many of them cannot conceive of nonviolence as a way of life, even a way of hatred and jealousy and fear. They do not recognize the element in human nature which grows proudly stronger in the face of hardship, of tragedy, of defeat, of insurmountable obstacles. They need to read of great human beings, not of failures and criminals; they need to understand, through reading, magnificent human values and strengths, not merely the ugly, small human sickness and evil to which we are all too frequently exposed in "life." Not all of us can be great men; there are very few models for humanity. But to know these few, to live in their minds, to experience their power is our only hope for fulfillment. And it is my peculiar task as an educator, I feel, to lead youth to these otherwise inaccessible human beings and ideas—to the dominion not of violence, but of excellence.

This is all simply to say that my perilous first year of teaching did not lead to the complete sacrifice of my ideals, as often seemed inevitable. Certainly my ideals, intellectual and moral, were challenged, suffered, altered and for a time appeared to be useless and therefore liable to permanent extinction. But when there have been enough bread and circuses, when all students are turned on but somehow still tuned out to a fulfilling, human way of living, then the dreams return. I never really got to these dreams this year; I never quite got past the first steps, the turning on, which cannot be neglected. But next year the first steps will be easier, will be the means rather than the end of my teaching. I probably didn't open a single door to that heady world of truth and beauty this year, but perhaps at least I managed to insist that it is out there somewhere. One of the most gratifying moments of the year was a student's parting promise, cryptic I suppose, but still a valid pleasure in my optimistic moments: "Well, I guess I'll keep reading this poetry now; I can't say that I've found the right poem for *me* yet, but I think there's one out there somewhere."

Exhaustion—the exhaustion from endless improvisation, endless emotional torment, all to violent plunges and flights between rational and emotional extremes—this was my overwheling reaction to this first year of teaching. Indeed there was shock—the shock of having a ninth-grade girl announce calmly to her homeroom teacher that she was tardy because she had slept with her boyfriend that night and, consequently, required an unexpected morning bath; and shock at the rage and disbelief I incited in an older student whom I had innocently befriended, when I tried to explain that the reason I wouldn't go out with him was that I was married, not that he was black. And I was often frustrated— when I used subject material too difficult or methods too boring, when class uproars prevented academic progress, when I had spent hours preparing a lesson the night before and nobody else in the class had read the assignment, when the audio-visual department refused to cooperate and confounded my plans for the day. Frustrations were endless, shocks enormously frequent! But beyond the shock and the frustration lay the final state: I was exhausted.

It had come at last—that day for which it seemed I had eternally longed. It was the end, the last day of school. How did it go—that rhyme? "No more pencils, no more books, no more teach— *students'* hostile looks." Yes, that old thing did have a merry ring to it! The students were not even coming that day; a few were scheduled to arrive bearing last-minute assignments, but I could see no possible complications. I had already computed most of my grades; I had cleaned out my desk, and, generally speaking, all was well! At ten o'clock—the final deadline— a few students dribbled in with hastily scrawled make-up work or slick excuses. At noon there were still two papers out, two which I had confidently expected. What should I do? Obviously these students were not planning to show up, as they had faithfully promised to do. Chillingly the truth of this year descended to dissipate my exhilaration. For the first time in my life I had allowed myself to be tortured, frustrated, disappointed, and deceived again and again by other people. I had in the final analysis not escaped this humiliation, but had rather been overtaken by it, with shattered pride and faded dreams. At times I had become demanding and shrewish at home, in reaction, no doubt, to the compulsory humility I had endured with uncharacteristic patience at school. I had continued against all the dictates of my rational mind to believe in students who made and broke promises with less concern than I might have given to breaking an empty jelly jar. And what, really, had I accomplished? (I was getting depressed again, which was poetically fitting, I guess, for this last day.) The two students with whom I had spent more than twenty-five hours in the last two or three weeks working individually to help them pass had promised to turn in written reports on the last day, and they hadn't even the concern to explain their delinquence. I had waited two hours past the time they were due, not allowing myself to entertain the suspicion that they weren't coming at all. Thank God I would not be back until September—until I had time to rejuvenate my jaded faith. Trying to control my disappointment, I assigned final grades and went up to the registrar's office to turn them in. Spying a red folder in my mailbox, I sheepishly, yet fearfully approached to find one of the two projects I had expected, dropped off at the wrong place, but faithfully there. I was ashamed of my hasty despair. What had I done this year? Where had I succeeded? Well, after all, fifty percent on this final day is not so bad. Of course next year I would have to try for seventy-five percent; but fifty percent is not so bad, I smiled.

Eleanor Fuke

Identity or Discipline

I have taught high school for only one year and already I know I don't want to do it again. The reasons have everything and nothing to do with the students I taught, and more than a little to do with the minus quality of my teaching.

This minus quality resulted in great part from my not having thought through my role as teacher before I entered the classroom. I had questions about the legitimacy of my role, and no answers. That is, I needed to know what there was inherent in me, twenty-three years old and knowing very little American history, and in the system that gave me the right to get up before 100 students for the next forty weeks and demand that they pay attention to me. It was my feeling, and it ran deeper than mere humility, that without this right, without something indispensable to offer my students, they might as well be the teachers and me the student. I had never felt this way while I was a student. I had had plenty of incompetent teachers whom I wished banished from the profession, but I had only questioned their competence, never their right to be there. Nor had I ever demanded—or expected—anything indispensable from them. Yet in the last few weeks of freedom before school began, I questioned the teacher-student authority relationship so searchingly, that the whole structure came crashing down around me, and I entered school thinking I had no right at all to be there. For some reason I didn't turn to anyone for help, and in consequence I continued to flounder right up until January. Now that school is over I find that had I read John Dewey's *Experience and Education,* I would have found precisely the answer I was looking for: simply, that the young in society have to be educated and that a teacher, by virtue of his or her training, knows more about his subject than his students do, regardless of their apparent sophistication or their knowledge of extracurricular subjects. I realize now that I was questioning the wrong thing—that all along I had been questioning the teacher's role and the legitimacy of his authority when I should have been concentrating on what and how to teach my classes.

Yet despite this search for identity as a teacher, I had no qualms about what I would teach. I was confident we had plenty to talk about, although I hadn't prepared anything specific. I suppose I expected daily classes to spring full-blown from the classroom air.

And so, following a final week of panic in which I prepared no classes because I was too nervous to do so, I faced my first day as a teacher. And if the unknown had been enough to panic' me, the reality of those first days was enough to terrify me. There they were, my first class, thirty-eight of them, and I had nothing to say. Suddenly my philosophical identity crisis no longer mattered. I had a much more pressing problem on hand—what to say right now, this instant! No matter what I thought of my right to be there, there I was, and thirty-eight bodies were waiting for me to begin. They were actually sitting patiently, waiting, *expecting* me to begin. So after all the soul-searching, there in front of me was the legitimacy of my "authority": thirty-eight students' expectations of their teacher.

Their expectations helped get me through my classes that day, but they didn't solve my original problem. I still wondered what kind of a lasting contribution I could make to their lives. This was not a narcissistic query, but one stemming from concern over public school education in this country. How can a high school teacher help educate her students, help make them more competent at living in this society? We all, in our more unrealistic moments, imagine ourselves as great leaders or great healers or great teachers, known to and beloved by the world for our courage, skill, and compassion. I had known for a long time that I would never achieve world renown for anything, but until I faced my first class, I had still thought I could be a great teacher.

I had had this confidence for several years. As a senior in high school I was sure anyone, including myself, could be better than my American history teacher. As a senior at Cornell University, I wanted to teach American history not to replace one teacher but to change an entire approach. I wanted to end the drudgery and concentrate on the historical bases of contemporary problems.

In June of 1965, immediately after graduation from college, I joined the West Tennessee Voters' Project. My perspective on American history changed again. The project had begun in the winter of 1963–64 at the Cornell University–Tompkins County (New York) Fund for Free and Fair Elections in Fayette County, Tennessee. Fayette County is the poorest county in Tennessee, and with a few outstanding exceptions its black residents (sixty-six percent of the total population) are demoralized.

The project workers were Negro residents and Cornell University students. Their object for the first summer (1964) was to insure an honest election. A Negro was running for county tax assessor and a white liberal for county sheriff. Neither man won his contest, but each carried some election districts and would have carried more had the election been fair. The story of the 1964 project is told in the book, *Step by Step: Evolution in Operation,* Cornell Students Civil Rights Program in Tennessee, edited by Douglas Dowd and Mary Nichols (New York: Norton, 1965).

In the summer of 1965, when I went to Tennessee, there was no election, but the project carried on. Renamed the West Tennessee Voters' Project, it strove to build a self-sustaining political organization that could nominate and elect Negroes to county offices. In addition to Fayette, its territory now included two adjoining counties, Haywood and Hardeman. My job took me from house to house—shack to shack, actually—in an attempt to convince people that their votes meant effective political power since they outnumbered the whites two to one.

We managed to strengthen the organization in some election districts, but on the whole the effort failed. In 1966 a few Negroes gained office in Fayette County, but the effort to coordinate Negro votes produced only short-run results.

The most valuable lesson of my five months with Fayette County residents was learning to view the world from the perspective of a different culture—learning to view it from the bottom up. It was a difficult life, but not intolerable. We got used to it. We knew we were working to change things, and of course, if things got too rough we could always go home. Nevertheless, even though I adjusted in a way to Fayette County, and despite the fact that the work had its rewards, I grew cynical about life in general and democratic government in particular. At the same time, I grew intolerant of my armchair liberal friends in the North who sat in comfort as they read my letters. As a result of my experiences, my concern was to incorporate into American history a realistic look at the oppressed groups in our society and at the mistakes the United States has made in dealing with oppressed populations of other countries.

I left Tennessee in November 1965, worked with the New York State Employment Agency as an employment interviewer for the New York City service industries, and entered the University of Chicago MAT program the next fall. The program requires a full year of teaching, and I chose to teach in a city school rather than a suburban one. I felt that the great educational problems lie in the cities, with students who could possibly "make it" in society with a good education. I also knew I would have greater curricular freedom in the city than in the suburbs, if only because the city board of education does not have the time, and the parents don't have the desire, to check on all the teachers.

I was assigned to a predominantly Negro school that had experienced "The Change" from white to black in the last four to five years. In the fall of 1967, when I entered, it was 95 percent black, and I had only 12 white students out of a total of 160. Eight of these were in my two senior contemporary history classes, and one in my junior history class. I had one white sophomore and one freshman in my study hall and in my freshman homeroom. This distribution reflected the racial pattern in the school as a whole, which was one of fewer and fewer white students in each succeeding freshman class.

Although the neighborhood was segregated, the school was not "inner city" in the sense of having tough students from broken, lower-class homes. Instead the neighborhood was lower middle class, with parents holding white collar jobs. The students usually lived in one-family houses with both their parents, and many seniors expected to go to college. The majority of the students held middle-class attitudes, supporting nonviolence and integration. It should be noted, however, that the economic level of the neighborhood was dropping, and with it the academic abilities of the incoming black students.

I had several things to offer my students—I enjoy teenagers, I enjoy American and world history and have ideas on how to make them interesting. In contemporary history classes I was willing to teach subjects that would interest them, such as the war in Vietnam, civil rights, and drugs. This willingness to approach them on their own terms gave me confidence that the students would accept me.

My method was simple enough: be the opposite to most public school teachers. Teach students, not subject matter. Teach them to reason and question what they see and hear, not to memorize and follow blindly. Give them material they would enjoy thinking about, and provide an atmosphere in which they could express themselves without fear of recrimination. But launching this program required a forceful and favorable impression the first day, and I had not prepared anything.

In fact, the bell had rung that day to begin my first class, and I was still wondering what to say to the thirty-eight contemporary history students who were gazing expectantly at me. When I could no longer procrastinate, I made a vain attempt to appear self-confident by telling myself I knew more about the year's course than they did (a lie); and taking a deep breath, I began. I have no idea what I said. I think I promised that they would learn something in my class if they kept their ears open, because I would give them interesting classes on subjects of interest to them. Whatever I said, I know I said it in forceful tones, and immediately afterward involved them in a discussion of why Chicago had had no riots during the summer. Looking back, I think I really impressed my contemporary history classes that day, especially the first one. I finished it by swearing just as the bell rang. I inadvertently referred to the Milwaukee riot as "all hell breaking loose." I was embarrassed, but they loved it.

Full of confidence from my debut, I went to my second class prepared for the same degree of success, and to my horror I met with bedlam. This was a world history class. Required for graduation, the course is usually peopled by juniors—that is, allegedly mature individuals—but here they were running around, talking, laughing, arguing, and yelling. The administration expected me to teach them something? They were out of their collective minds. I had clearly met my match. With no combat training, I was at a loss to know what to do. Periods were thirty-five minutes each that day, and thirty had passed before there was anything like order in the room. Even then it was not order, only something like it. And the way I achieved that much was to discuss again the absence of summer riots in Chicago. They were all interested in this, contributing their ideas willingly whenever they were able to hear. But I had to forego taking attendance and seating and making "introductory remarks." I left the room shaken, well aware that here lay my greatest challenge.

The next two periods were for lunch and guidance, which later turned out to be a euphemism for a much needed R. and R. My third and final class met seventh period, an unfortunate time of day for all of us who hold that early afternoons are for sleeping. Not only is this my own personal credo, but it seemed I had a whole roomful of agreeing seniors. They proved to be a very friendly group when Melissa's (a white girl) racial hostilities weren't showing, but it was always a chore to get them moving. And I didn't always manage to.

The fourth period debacle had underscored my apprehensions about discipline. From the start—indeed, well before I entered a classroom—I knew that discipline would be a problem for me. From past experience with teenagers I expected to establish rapport with a good portion of my students, but I also feared that when a conflict arose it would develop into a full-scale problem that I would not know how to handle. I was sure that a few students would see through my facade of self-confidence from the first moment and defy me on the spot—get up and walk out, perhaps, or walk around the room talking to other students, in complete disregard of everything I said.

Compounding these fears were my previously-mentioned doubts about the rightfulness of my authority. Not only was I concerned lest students disregard my commands, I was suspicious that they would be right to do so.

Much to my relief I had no major discipline problems, not even in fourth period, and with some curiosity I noted why. The reason certainly was not that I had a magnetic personality students couldn't help but respond to, but rather that they had been conditioned to obey. Considering my complete inability to say "boo" during those first days, I was thankful; but as I grew more secure in my authority, I realized that this obedience was a fault as well as a virtue. The fault came when it was apathy or blind obedience rather than obedience stemming from respect for either the teacher or the command.

I noticed the conditioning most in my homeroom students. Freshman homerooms assembled the first day in the lunch room. There was no order to the table assignments, which left us milling around for untold exasperating minutes trying to find our assigned seats. As I searched for homeroom 237, I watched with dread the cocky ones with their brazen voices and self-assured strides, and with a sick feeling in my stomach I accepted the fact that they were probably all in my homeroom. What a shock, then, to find my freshmen huddled around the homeroom 237 sign, too scared even to talk to their few friends from elementary school. Their meekness did wonders for my self-confidence, and I allowed myself to indulge in the possibility that I would not be a total failure after all.

Despite the fact that I had no *major* discipline problems, I still didn't have good control over my classes, especially over the juniors. Before school began I had decided to pursue a course of "discipline from within." It would work this way: I would provide materials so interesting that the students would rather pay attention to them than talk to each other. Instead of me, then, it would be students who got annoyed with the talkers and who would make them be quiet. This would be all to the good, not only from a theoretical standpoint, but from the practical one of my authority problems as well (it was the twenty-first week of school before I could tell anyone to be quiet without having an identity crisis).

The flaws in this scheme were legion, but principally two: first, it required me to be perennially scintillating, which I am not; and second, I did not devise an alternative for the case of a class which would not respond to this kind of treatment. And of course I had just such a group: my fourth period world history class.

That class had such possibilities—and such problems! They ranged in ability from Tommy, functional illiterate, to Michael and Jon, who should have been in the next higher track. In between were people like Doreen, who could neither read nor write very well, but who contributed a great deal to class discussions; Charles, whose low grades and disinterest implied boredom with material he considered beneath him; Salinda, as poor as Doreen in skills, but who substituted constant chatter for Doreen's insight; Joyce, who stopped coming after ten weeks; Carol, whose daily greeting was, "Do I have to come to class today?"; Kenneth, who had latent ability, but who did nothing but clown all year; and Joe, who tried so hard to improve his skills, but never quite learned to distinguish between the important and the unimportant. Each of these required a different approach and much individual attention, and I was at a loss to provide either one.

This is the only class I would like to do over. Given a second chance, I would walk in on the first day and lay down ground rules about noise and conduct in the room. I would then strictly enforce them, despite the suspension or psychological effects that could result from an interview with a counselor or the disciplinarian. Veteran teachers assured me that I would only have to send one student to the office once, and I would have no more problems. As it was, I was determined to protect them from both suspension and harmful psychological effects, certain that I would win them over with my self-discipline scheme. It took me twenty weeks to admit I was wrong and to attempt to enforce quiet. Naturally at that late date the attempt was not particularly successful. Nor did I try very hard. I would move them, separate them, chide them, talk to them individually or in groups, but never send them to the disciplinarian. Once or twice I simply sat down behind the desk, took out some papers, and began to read, ignoring both their chatter and their entreaties to answer questions and continue the class. One time was the review day before the mid-term exam. This turned out to be a most effective ploy. Instead of reviewing, they talked, so I sat down—to their great consternation. When they got themselves quieted down, it took only a few pointed words to show them why we had progressed so slowly during the year.

Undoubtedly there was some ego involved here, of the "I don't want them to dislike me, so I won't discipline them or give them any bad grades" kind. This line of reasoning is bunk, of course, but I'm speaking from a June perspective, not a September or a January one.

Not wanting to incriminate myself, I disregarded my study hall when counting up disciplinary successes and failures. This study hall defies description: it had to be lived through to be believed. Overcrowding of the school required that the lunch room be used as a study. The lunchroom is huge, an excellent place for tag, penny pitching (illegal) and wrestling. No matter how many teachers there were, there were always corners far enough away to go at it for a minute or two. If this were not enough, the eighth period group of 100 to 150 freshmen—my group—had been left without supervision for the first six days of school. And on the seventh day, who was put in to supervise it but two women, both of us nondisciplinary types. This is not the way to bring order out of chaos. We sized up the situation in a glance and agreed to keep the students from running, shouting, fighting, and killing one another. This was an effective and, I think, appropriate modus operandi, which the school disciplinarian spoiled by insisting on rigidly enforced quiet. We laughed, a little hysterically perhaps, and made up a seating chart which the students promptly ignored. Once we had given the studious a chance to transfer to a quiet study hall, we regressed to a policy of live and let live.

Several weeks later the principal divided the study into three groups and transferred them to the auto shop, the teachers' lunch room, and an empty classroom. I was assigned the classroom and, wonder of wonders, kept my charges quiet and, in some cases, doing their homework—for about two weeks. Then I began to accumulate more students than I could handle (I found I could keep eighteen quiet), and the noise level began to rise. Theoretically I had several options open to me. I could have sent them to their counselor for a little talk, which the counselor would enter on their permanent record. Or if their behavior were particularly disruptive, I could have filled out a disciplinary card—a very serious step which would have resulted in a suspension and an entry on their permanent record—and have sent them to the disciplinarian. Unfortunately I had seen enough of "heart-to-heart talks" between counselors and students to know I did not want to subject my freshmen and sophomores to them. And a disciplinary card and suspension for talking in study hall? Ridiculous!

I wasn't aiming for dead quiet. I would much have preferred the chance to talk with the students, as I had talked with one of them, John Murray, when study hall was in the lunchroom. John and most of the others in this study were not the scholars of their years. In study hall they either talked or stared out the window. No books, no homework, no studying, just aimless mind wandering. Perhaps a few of these were incapable of much school work, but the majority had simply been left behind in first grade when they hadn't learned to read. Now, like John, they were waiting for their sixteenth birthday and the chance to escape from school by dropping out.

The friendly atmosphere with minimal noise lasted for another couple of weeks. During this time I allowed a game of matchbook football at my desk (it's a good thing the principal didn't know this; he had outlawed chess in another study hall), in which John and Walter, a white sophomore, took part. After several days the game broke up, but Walter continued to sit up in front near my desk and chatter at me. I didn't attach any significance to this, as John and others had done the same in the past. One afternoon I was embarrassed to overhear a remark about white Walter being the white teacher's pet. I was constrained to ask him to move into one of the rows with everyone else, which he did only under protest. He never forgave me for it, either, which made me sad. While he got along perfectly well with the black students in the study, apparently he resented being knocked from his position of superiority and being made equal with everyone else. At least, so I imagine—he wouldn't speak to me the rest of the time he remained in the study, though several times I caught him staring at me.

Just about this same time I had another influx of students, and with them came a second teacher to help control things. She was appalled at my laxness, and I reluctantly agreed to help her establish control over the group. The effort failed. Not only was I an unwilling partner in the crackdown, not only had they gone without discipline for seven or eight weeks, but they knew I would never send them to their counselor or to the disciplinarian, and would never fill out a disciplinary card on any of them, not even on the terror of the group. Happily, he didn't appear too often, though I was sorry his absences were due to frequent suspensions.

Naturally the students took advantage of this leniency, not maliciously, not in a "let's-put-one-over-on-them" way, just noisily. It wasn't until spring that the other teacher came up with the idea of calling parents to inform them of their child's noisiness in study hall and to ask them to speak to their son or daughter about it. Surprisingly enough, this was a most effective measure. In the meantime each of us had occasionally tried to instill some reality into the more aimless ones. But at that age one isn't thinking of one's fifty to sixty years of future and the best ways to prepare for it. It's still very unreal and far away. Not until the middle of junior year, around the sixteenth birthday, when one decides whether to stay in school or to drop out, does the possibility of adult failure begin to strike home. And then suddenly all sorts of people want to go to college.

Of course for some the sixteenth birthday comes in the sophomore year, or even the freshman, and they just drop out right then or are expelled as trouble makers. These are the ones with the least hope for themselves—the John Murrays who know they're already failures because of all the times they've been held back in school. Usually they're not "bad" or even rebellious, just thoughtless or bewildered, as in the case of Thomas Hunt.

Thomas was a charming, mischievous, thoughtless, carefree-acting fifteen-year-old freshman. He wanted to finish high school and become a lawyer, but his grades ranged from a high of D to a majority of F's, and he was rarely out of trouble. Usually the trouble was for being late to school and to his classes (automatic suspension for so many tardies, which may be rescinded if a parent comes to school, but most parents work during the day). Once it was for smoking on school grounds, once on the suspicion of doing so, and once for pulling a false fire alarm while leaving the building during one of the school-wide disturbances set off by an earlier false alarm. He also drank in school, for something daring to do (he once proudly showed me a bottle of gin in his locker), but I never heard that he was caught for it. Pulling the fire alarm resulted in a twenty-day suspension—that is, twenty school days —which to a failing student is like saying, "Don't bother to return this semester; these extra twenty days out of school automatically assure you of a failure-for-absence this semester, not to mention the academic one you are sure to get because of all the work you will have missed." It's no wonder Thomas was bewildered. And not understanding how the game is played, Thomas didn't play. The result is that he will be a prime target for expulsion as soon as he turns sixteen, not only because he is so often in trouble, but also because the school is overcrowded and the administration doesn't know how to deal with him.

I don't know how I would have reacted to Thomas had I had him in a class. In class one is normally too busy concentrating on the students in relation to the material being presented, to focus much attention on the students in relation to themselves. As it was, Thomas was in my study hall, which, the way I ran it, gave me ample opportunity to come to know him. And yet what did I do for him except lend him moral support in his trials with The System? I am sure that, could someone magically confer upon Thomas the ability to read and write and manage the other necessary learning skills, he would become a passable student really interested in school. Instead he is on the outside looking in, and all because he failed to learn the basic skills in primary school and no one has had the time to teach them to him in high school. Of course reading and writing are not Thomas's only problems. The point is simply that if Thomas were not a failure in school, he might be able and willing to devote more time to his problems at home and perhaps untangle some of them. And no doubt he wouldn't wander the halls for a good portion of the day, either.

My leniency didn't stop with discipline; it extended into academics as well. It's not that I didn't make assignments, but that I didn't enforce their due dates and I didn't grade them right away. The result: mass confusion and multi-headaches. I wanted adult behavior from my students and refused to hound them for their overdue work; I let them hand it in late, sometimes very late indeed. All this did was encourage them not to do it at all until the last week before grades were due. Because I didn't grade their papers right away (how could I demand they hand theirs in on time if I didn't return them shortly thereafter?), I didn't always know for certain whether or not a particular claimant had handed in his paper.

Nor did I give out as many warning notices as I should have. Failure warnings are issued to students and parents a few weeks before grades are due, and are prerequisite to a failing grade. By June several of my students had worked themselves into F grades, but by then it was too late to do anything about it. Anyone who deserved to fail the whole year had also deserved to fail in January and again in March, but since I had not warned or failed them then, I could not suddenly fail them at the end of the year.

I had reasons for much of this leniency. Some were compassionate, others misguided; but except for not grading papers right away, my actions were actual policies with me. I didn't always carry them out very well, but I was trying to combine humanness with authority. As I see it now, I should have spent more time in the beginning establishing my authority.

One reason I didn't try very hard to correct any of my mistakes was that all year long my mind was elsewhere than on my teaching. I was engaged, and from October to June my fiancé was in Washington, D.C. His absence made me lonely and miserable and affected my work more than I care to admit. Intellectually I knew I could best forget my loneliness by becoming absorbed in my work, and the few times I did devote whole evenings to planning lessons or grading papers were the times I was happiest and had the greatest feeling of accomplishment. And of course the days following those energetic evenings went well because I had prepared for them. But for some masochistic reason I rarely operated that way. All year long I was pulled in conflicting directions in my effort to make the time pass as quickly and as painlessly as possible until June, when school was to end and my fiancé was to return. The whole first semester I fought school, hating to go each day, heaving a great sigh of relief at the end of the day, and doing as little work as possible at night. My reasoning was that school was a terrible pressure and that the after school hours were far more pleasant because no demands were made on me then. Yet the time from 4:00 P.M., when I arrived home, to 8:00 A.M. the next morning, when I left again for school, was actually worse. No matter how enthusiastic I had become during the day, and no matter how eagerly I rushed home to get started on some new idea, I had only to open the door to my apartment to have loneliness replace my enthusiasm. Instead of preparing lessons and grading papers, as I had looked forward to only minutes before, my reaction was to shove it all out of sight, out of mind, and read a Georgette Heyer novel until 3 o'clock in the morning. By November I was ready to quit my job and join my fiancé in Washington. This was impractical financially and academically—it would have meant foregoing my degree. My fiancé was ready to have me move to Washington and become a secretary, but of course I didn't want to be a secretary; I wanted to be a teacher.

My advisor hit upon what sounded like the ideal solution. To relieve some of the pressure, he suggested I use only already-prepared materials. So far I had been creating my own course materials. These I would painfully extract from scholarly books on the subject in question, and then edit down to the vocabulary level of a particular class. Such an attempt at creativity didn't always stem from a reformist zeal; often there simply were no materials available on the subjects I wanted to teach and my students wanted to study. The students suffered a double handicap in this respect. Not only were there no materials already prepared, but I am not an especially creative person, and what I came up with on my own wasn't the most stimulating work.

My advisor's plan, then, wasn't such a good one after all. To follow it, we would have had to forget about drugs and other current topics, because there just are no materials available in cheap, easy-to-read, multiple copies; and I stress the need for all those gratifications: cheap, easy-to-read, and multiple copies.

And so I was no better off than before, although I felt better from having had a sympathetic ear, but by assigning a library project to my two senior classes I at least got them off my back and could comfortably retreat into my private misery until Thanksgiving vacation enabled me to go to Washington' for a few days.

Suddenly, in January, I did a complete about-face, and instead of hating school I began hating being at home. All at once it dawned on me that I enjoyed school. To my great surprise, I found myself looking forward to it. It was more interesting than my after-school life, as there was more variety to the people and the activities, and so the time passed more quickly than at home.

Even so, the quality of my teaching didn't improve, and I never became deeply involved in school affairs or with any of my students. I held myself aloof, jealous of demands on my time and on my emotions, as though protecting myself, from what, I didn't know. The aloofness was also in part a reaction against one of the teachers most actively concerned with his students. I didn't like him, and unfortunately for me, active involvement with the school and the students usually meant active involvement with him.

And so I vacillated, torn between wanting to be in school so the time would pass quickly and wanting to be out of school because I wasn't doing anything worthwhile in class. To be honest, I can't remember anything we did in any of my classes from January to June. The students probably can't, either, and the question is, was it as boring and depressing for them as it often was for me? Oh, I can remember the topics we covered second semester, but what puzzles me is, how did we pass the time from day to day? What did we *do* for forty minutes each day???

One reason I can't recall more academically about those long, dark days is that everything was overshadowed by racial tensions among the faculty and student body. I had had a foretaste in September and October when we studied slavery in all three of my classes. My white seniors did not appreciate the study. Some were hostile, others studiously avoided contact with their black classmates. Never uttering a word in class about their feelings, they gave vent to them on paper. Sam, in contemporary history class, asked sarcastically if this were "a contemporary American history class or an African history class. If it is a contemporary history class, I will be expected to have a thorough understanding of contemporary America. At the rate we're going, I'm afraid we won't have this understanding." This raised some speculation in my mind about Sam's parents, although it was secondary to my concern over his hostility.

I knew I should talk to the white students to find out how hostile they were, towards whom and why. It seemed they did not view race as one of our most contemporary problems. I admit I was uncomfortable to meet them face to face in the situation, and I was ashamed of myself for this cowardice. One of the white students attacked me once on paper, accusing me of "using [my] position as teacher to brainwash the white students into thinking they owe the Negro something." I in no way wanted to expose myself to further attack by appearing to rush to my own defense, so I let it go, and in so doing let the majority rule without allowing minority rights. Because we changed topics, the hostility died; but I knew it would reappear in the spring when we were to study civil rights.

In fact, racial hostility flared again much sooner than I had expected, but not just among my students. In January and February a series of incidents brought to the fore latent teacher-student and teacher-teacher conflict over student-centered and racial issues. Much of the antagonism was directed toward the Afro-American Club. The club had sprung up that fall at the initial request of two girls and met with widespread acceptance among the student body, although membership during the first few months was low.

Six teachers sponsored it, among them three black teachers and three of the four white University of Chicago beginning teachers. One of the black teachers, Mrs. Jackson, was the formal head and bore the brunt of the faculty and administration attacks. Everything ran smoothly until the club members voted in January to display some race pride by having an Afro-American Day. On this day everyone was invited to wear African dress to school. Everyone who did so enjoyed the day tremendously, and that week's Afro-American Club meeting was one of the largest of the year.

But the Afro-American Day aroused antagonism from white students who thought that African clothes were inappropriate in school, and they regarded this recognition of Afro-Americanism as a threat to their already uncomfortable minority situation. Several white students, mine among them, took their grievance to the principal, who was unsuccessful in allaying their fears.

Many teachers protested, too, and all of us in the Afro-American Club were aware that their arguments constituted an oblique attack on the existence of the club, as well as one against Afro-American Day. The club is not popular among the older teachers. Its members believe in Black Power, something which many whites and Negroes distrust or fear. Despite a school newspaper article explaining Black Power as Black pride and as an attempt to achieve individual and group success in society through the pride, some students and teachers insisted that the club stood for, or at least condoned, militancy and violence, and they felt a psychological and physical threat from its continued existence.

To complicate matters, a student-run underground newspaper called the *Rocking Horse* made its debut not only in the heat of the Afro-American Day controversy, but also during an argument with the faculty sponsor-editor of the regular school newspaper over space for articles on Afro-American history, poems by members of the Afro-American club, and so on. Because of the timing of its arrival coincidentally with these disputes, and because most of the *Rocking Horse* staff were also club members, faculty members opposed to either the paper or the club sought to discredit both by branding the paper as the voice of the Afro-American Club. Their "proof" came in the second issue, when Mrs. Jackson's name and mine appeared in the paper as its faculty sponsors. Arousing further ire were several cartoons in obviously bad taste.

The appearance of a second issue of the upstart publication, together with our names and the cartoons, caused a terrific uproar. One teacher was particularly incensed over my apparent endorsement of the cartoons. She demanded to know if University of Chicago students were so accustomed to obscenity that it no longer bothered us. I hated to appease an avowed opponent of the club, but had to. The *Rocking Horse* staff, knowing of Mrs. Jackson's and my sympathy with them, had taken the liberty of using our names without our knowledge. I had to admit further that the cartoons offended us, too, and that had we actually been the sponsors we would not have allowed all of them to be included.

The quality of writing in the *Rocking Horse* caused further turmoil. Few teachers or administrators could believe our school harbored students with so much ability. The teacher mentioned above accused the club sponsors of ghost writing; the principal suggested that some teacher must have helped out, at least a bit.

The *Rocking Horse* crisis ended just in time for an Afro-American assembly, held in February during Afro-American History Week. The club invited two popular Black Chicago personalities, Joyce Aaron and William Lewis, to address the students. Lewis read selections from his Black poetry, and Miss Aaron gave a talk centering on the question of Black identity. The combination of bad acoustics, an inferior address system, and a seat under the balcony kept me and my homeroom students from hearing anything but snatches of the program. I could only see—and hear—the students cheer Miss Aaron time and again.

I was disappointed not to have heard the program, but I need not have been, for my juniors and seniors were only too eager to fill me in. So was the faculty, whose response was just as negative as the students' was positive. Few faculty members had anything good to say. Most deplored the way Miss Aaron had "stirred up" the students, and were too shocked and outraged over the language and ideas in Lewis's poetry to do any more than splutter. No one claimed that the students were not familiar with his four-letter words, but all agreed that a school should not condone them. Many students agreed with this but did not get as worked up. They got upset with the teachers who had walked out of the assembly in protest.

Miss Aaron's remarks caused even more of an outcry. At one point she declared, "I am an African by descent and an American by force." This the faculty deplored, as they claimed it stirred up hate and emphasized the students' blackness and hence their differentness from white people. She also asserted that history teachers were not fulfilling their assigned roles unless they taught Afro-American students Afro-American history. Furthermore, she told the students, if their teachers were not doing this, they should demand it. This last was too much for most of the faculty, for it called on the students to question the system and, in questioning, possibly to destroy it. In essence Miss Aaron was commanding them to challenge their teachers' authority. Nothing, the teachers felt, could come of this but disciplinary chaos.

Something quite different came of it in my classes. On the day following the assembly my normally dead-headed seventh period class carried on a heated but absorbing discussion of Miss Aaron's ideas. It was the most exciting class of the year. Not only did the students openly confront each other, but throughout most of the period they were so engrossed—all but Gertrude—that they forgot me entirely and crowded about the principal arguers. I did only two things: I periodically asked the boy with the loudest voice in the class to quiet the room so we all could hear, and I tried to talk some sense and manners into Gertrude.

Gertrude was glib, and an admitted racist. Throughout the discussion she persisted in telling the world at large that the whole thing was "revolting," and asked if I would please excuse her from the room before she got sick. Rarely do I get angry, but Gertrude earned herself a regular tirade that day. Frank and Bruce, two white boys sitting nearby, also got an earful. After Gertrude admitted that race and poverty are our two greatest domestic problems, I explained that since she attended a virtually all-black school, she was on the "inside," so to speak, and in a position to learn what it was all about simply by paying attention to her fellow students and what they were saying. "No one," I concluded, "is asking you to sympathize with anything you hear, but if you demand the right to call yourself educated, then it is imperative that you understand the issues involved. If you would keep your ears open, you would realize that you have a unique opportunity to begin reaching such an understanding. And if you don't take that opportunity, you can rightfully be called ignorant." Gertrude started listening. Of the two white boys, Frank had always been affable with everyone and did not need my lecture, but

I am inclined to think my words had little or no impact on Bruce. Gertrude had a bigger shock in store than my tirade. Toward the end of class a quiet boy got up and asked her point blank why she and some of her white friends had gone directly from the assembly to the principal to complain. I do not know who was more surprised, Gertrude or myself. One thing is certain: it was the most valuable question anyone asked all year. Taken off guard, and faced with a group inclined to be intolerant of such action, Gertrude at first would not answer, claiming instead that her office visit had been on school newspaper business (she was editor). Why she changed her mind I will never know, but she did, and with little apparent uneasiness began to explain the white students' attitude on the assembly. "It's not that we think you shouldn't have your rights," she began, and was almost drowned out by groans. "We agree with your goals, but didn't like the way either Joyce Aaron or William Lewis presented their ideas, because it seemed they were trying to stir up hate with all their talk of Black Power. We went to the principal to find out just what you mean by Black Power." Later in the period she admitted that she and her friends felt threatened by so much talk of Black Power, but that after meeting with the principal and several teachers, they had emerged with a much greater understanding and a new definition.

I am cynical enough to have suspected Gertrude of being more glib than honest in revealing her new understanding, but a chance remark made me reconsider. Another girl asked her with some hostility why she had gone to the principal with her questions instead of to her parents. With a shrug she answered that her parents would never understand. A typical teenage response, but not from a student whose parents' opinions on race had come through time and again on her papers. We all, even Gertrude, perhaps, were sorry when the bell cut short our discussion. We hoped to continue it the next day, but Gertrude, Frank, and Bruce, were all conspicuously absent. The black students accepted their absence with little comment, but the class was a dull one.

Pam, a white senior in third period, was also absent that day and for a few days following, and her classmates took it with far less grace than did the seventh period group. As it turned out, Pam and Gertrude, and possibly Frank and Bruce as well, were talking with the principal about Black Power and their own position in the school during these periods. None of us knew that, the first day of Pam's absence, and Tony demanded to know if I wasn't going to fail Pam because of her cutting and all the work she was missing. I tried not to show the amusement I felt as I reminded him that Pam was not an habitual cutter, was rarely absent, and was an A student as well, and in no danger of failing. These considerations didn't weigh very heavily with most of the class, but when we found out where Pam had been, we talked about reasons why she had not turned to her classmates for answers. We had never taken the trouble to create an atmosphere in which she would feel free to ask her questions and air her doubts.

When Pam returned a few days later, she did answer a question or two about the white students' thoughts at this time, but it was a stilted discussion and we did not pursue the matter with her. An interesting sidelight was the reaction of Joanne, a blind senior, to the racial tensions. She had been blind since birth, and while I was curious to know how she perceived color and race, I did not come to know her well enough to feel free to ask her about it. She shed some light on it herself, inadvertently, on one of the days Pam was absent. Knowing by then that Pam was talking with the principal about Black Power and white students, we were discussing why it was she had shied away from talking to the class about it. I remarked that not only was Pam shy by nature, she was also the only white student in the class now that the two white boys had dropped out. This could not help but be an uncomfortable position for her since she was so unaccustomed to it. Suddenly I realized several girls nearby were trying to get my attention. "Miss Doyle, Miss Doyle," they whispered, "you're forgetting Joanne. She's white, too, you know." Joanne and I were both embarrassed, and I laughingly apologized, explaining that I had trouble thinking of her in a racial way. Later in the period we had moved onto discussion of a rumor that the white students now wanted to have a dress-up day of their own. It turned out to be groundless, but at the time it angered the black students, who didn't stop to think about the clothes one would wear to a "White Day." Trying to get them to explain the reasons for their anger, I asked them what difference it would make if the white students did have a dress-up day. At this Joanne's hand shot up, and she answered, full of indignation, "Because *they're* the minority" (emphasis hers). I'm sure the black students didn't catch the irony of her pronoun, because they all chorused their agreement, but Joanne and I were both amused by it, and she admitted after class that the "they're" had slipped out unconsciously.

The next racial episode was February 21, the third anniversary of Malcolm X's assassination, when Kenneth, president of the Afro-American Club, and a couple of his friends planned a walkout. The original idea came from a group called A Fair Defense for Black Students, an independent student group operating among the city's high school students to insure fair treatment of students by teachers and administrators. Unfortunately for all concerned, Kenneth didn't decide that the school should join the walkout until the day before, when it was too late to organize anything. As a result the idea fell into the wrong minds, and it appeared by that afternoon that there would be rowdy disturbances the next day instead of an orderly demonstration. Realizing this, the student leadership of the Afro-American Club met and went to the principal to explain what had happened and to request that he send out a memo the next morning to the effect that the walkout had been called off. The principal declined to do this, trusting instead in his students not to walk out.

In a way, he was right: few students actually did walk out. But a false fire alarm between third period and homeroom, a coterie of boys racing madly through the halls during homeroom and overturning the tall metal trash cans, myriads of police cars outside the building and many uniformed officers inside, lunchroom speeches by students and faculty urging students not to walk out, and small fires intentionally set in washroom waste cans provided confusion throughout the day.

Even so, in the opinion of students I knew, there would have been no major disturbance and no need to dismiss school early had the police not entered the lunchroom and forcibly removed a student standing on a table speaking about Malcolm X and encouraging students to walk out. From what I can gather, few students were paying attention to what he was saying, if only because they couldn't hear him. But as soon as the police entered the scene, everyone paid close attention. In the ensuing melee several students were hit, not only by police, but also by chairs, plates, and cups aimed at the police by infuriated students.

Student reaction to the day was mixed. My seniors and juniors were nearly unanimous in denouncing the whole affair and the unknown students who were at the bottom of it, not necessarily because they were against the idea of commemorating Malcolm X, but because the whole thing had been botched up. Unanimous, too, was their anger with the police and with the administration for calling in the police. I don't know where my freshman study hall and homeroom students stood on the issue, but most faculty and upperclassmen agreed that it was the younger ones who regarded the day as a picnic, while the older students debated among themselves the merits of a walkout as the most appropriate way to commemorate Malcolm X, and even whether Malcolm X was the most appropriate Afro-American to commemorate. I went a step further and discussed with my classes the ways to, and the ways not to, organize a demonstration in order to have it be a success.

Our public image was not helped by the fact that students from a white suburban school were visiting that day and that, lest they get hurt or lost, they were locked in the social room until their busses could come and "rescue" them. Locked in the room with them were several of our own white students. "Several" at Donner High doesn't mean too many, since the whites had totaled only five percent of the student population in September, and this percentage had dwindled during second semester as parents pulled their children out of what appeared to be a racially troubled school.

Soon after February 21 I noticed a list of history teachers on the blackboard in the history department office. The names were in three categories labeled "Yes," "Maybe," and "No." Aside from noting a certain division among the members of the three groups on racial and school issues. I didn't understand the breakdown. Responsible for the list were two white students who assisted the history department chairman and more or less ran the office, and they cheerfully explained the lists to me. It seems that at the height of the day's disturbance, when the police had invaded the lunchroom, a couple of elderly white teachers had locked themselves and their classes into their classrooms. The two white students had been in such classes and had decided that in the event of another such occurrence they should barricade the history department/audio-visual aids office and allow in only white students and those teachers known to be "safe." Hence the

lists. Needless to say, the elderly white teachers were all "Yeses."
I was a "Maybe."

Despite this, there was little racial trouble among students because so few of them were white; the real problems lay within
the faculty.

From the perspective of two teachers' meetings where teachers
chose their seats with an eye to clique solidarity, it seems there
were several groups within the faculty. The first and most in-
fluential with the administration was a group of older white
teachers, principally women. They had lived through several
ethnic changes in the school in their fifteen to forty years of teaching there, and were uncomfortable with the racial change of the
last four to five years. With them in attitude were a few young
white teachers, both men and women. The members of the other
very clearly defined group were young, black and white, male
and female, and liberal to radical in their views on discipline, on
the kinds of student activities the school should foster, and on the
extent to which students should have a say in running school
activities and disciplinary procedures. Naturally these two groups
were at loggerheads over issues such as Black Power and the
Afro-American Club.

In between were at least two other faculty groups: those—all
black—who criticized the "radicals" out of a genuine concern for
the issues involved, and those who took little or no vocal interest
but, in any conflict, generally sided with the conservative group.
It is hard to say who caused us more frustration, the older teachers
(and office clerical staff) who were stonily set against us, or the
black teachers who thought the Afro-American Club was basically a good idea but who found flaws in the way we were carrying it out.

Inevitably the radicals were blamed for stirring up all the
trouble we had that year. Listening to the office clerks the Monday
after Dr. Martin Luther King's assassination, one would believe
the young white beginning teachers had caused school to be let
out at 10:30 that morning.

In the words of some others, the blame for school problems lay
with the Afro-American Club sponsors and members.

In either case, these kinds of accusations pointed up a fundamental lack of understanding among faculty members: we, the
younger, more radical group, held that the disturbances were

symptomatic, and not the actual problem; that they were part of a larger, nation-wide and even world-wide pattern of student unrest; and that the blame for them could not be laid at the feet of any one person or group. The older faculty, on the other hand, held to a form of conspiracy theory about us: that we had come to Donner for the sole purpose of stirring up the race issue among students who would never have thought of it on their own. The young white faculty didn't appreciate us, either, although they didn't go to such lengths in their disapproval. They just considered us troublemakers.

The two faculty meetings mentioned earlier were held in January and February, the first after the Afro-American assembly, and the second on February 21, the day of the walk-out. Both should have been scheduled as forums for discussing racial problems in the school and the best ways to handle them. Instead the first one was called by popular demand to discuss the types of assemblies that are proper for young people. And while the agenda of the second meeting was a small-group discussion of racial problems in the school, it happened to coincide with the Malcolm X disturbance, and we ended up meeting to discuss how to handle the next day of school. At that meeting I suggested we hold student-faculty workshops to give students a chance to air their grievances to the teachers and administration and possibly —hopefully—to give the faculty and administration an insight into the students' ideas and problems. This idea implied that students had some legitimate complaints about the way Donner was run and about the way teachers treated them, and the scattered applause that greeted my proposal was countered by such responses as "But I already know what my students are thinking," or "Definitely not, we're not going to let the students dictate to us how to run this school," and in hurt tones, "I can't imagine what she means. I've always enjoyed the greatest rapport with my students. We get along just fine." The warning that if we adults didn't listen to our students we would have even greater problems to solve elicited similar kinds of responses.

We didn't hold workshops then and we continued to have trouble. The trouble was always signaled by the fire alarm, rung either during homeroom or between third period and homeroom, both of which are times of optimum confusion, especially in a school lacking a public address system. This system worked like a charm, because no one ever knew if the alarm was real or false and whether or not they should clear the building. There is a state law requiring the building to be cleared in all instances of fire alarms, whether false or real, but it was virtually impossible for any teacher under 200 pounds to enforce it. Further, not all teachers wanted to go all the way down two or three flights of stairs for what they were certain was a prank. The resulting confusion was the first step to early dismissal. After the fire engines arrived and the washroom fires were put out and the all-clear sounded, if it looked as though things might settle down, there was bound to be a second alarm. Invariably most students would simply go home this time in order to avoid possible violence at school.

Sadly, one of these series of alarms sounded the day after Martin Luther King's assassination, and deprived the freshmen and sophomores of a moving memorial service. The juniors and seniors had just gone to the memorial assembly, and the freshmen and sophomores were on their way to homeroom to await their turn (we always had to have two assemblies in order to fit everyone in) when the fire alarm began. The result? The juniors and seniors proceeded with the service while the freshmen and sophomores, who most needed such a memorial to calm them down, were gaily at home long before the first assembly ended.

I missed what little school there was Monday because I had spent the weekend in Washington, D.C., and didn't want to face the drive from the airport into the restless South Side alone on Sunday night. I predicted I would not be missing much at school that day, as there was bound to be trouble of one sort or another and I was sure classes would be dismissed. There was, and they were, and I was not sorry to have missed it.

Fire alarms were the cause of all four early dismissals that year, including the one I missed the Monday after Dr. King's death. Tuesday was Dr. King's funeral, so there was no school. Wednesday we anticipated more trouble and another early dismissal, but finally, to our great relief, the principal had come up with a solution. It may be infallible, too, as the students at the city's worst high school have not been able to crack it. From that day forward we were completely to disregard any and all fire alarms. Should one be sounded, the building would be checked and, if there were a fire, the passing bell on the clock would be rung manually from the office.

This put an end to early dismissals, but it did not give the students a chance to tell the faculty and administration what was on their minds. As usual, we had dealt with a symptom instead of the problem.

On May 23, three months and two early dismissals after the original suggestion, we had our workshops. These were very effectively run by the human relations department of the Board of Education. The teachers and students met separately, each group with a board member. In the student groups the board representative was only an observer and note-taker, while in the faculty groups he was a discussion leader as well. The purpose was to air and discuss grievances of any and all types. The board members would then compile a report and make suggestions to the administration.

From many discussions in my three classes during the year, I knew that students were concerned with a whole range of issues, beginning with lunchroom prices and service and the two-dollar student activity fee. This fee covered the cost of printing the school newspaper (which no one liked particularly, because there were no articles of current interest, such as activities in the black community or on African history, or reports of Afro-American Club meetings); an I.D. card without even so much as a picture to give it some semblance of worth; a few not-so-interesting assemblies (and one terrific one with Sammy Davis, Jr., who had recently gone "Afro" and pro–Black Power, changes which shocked not a few faculty and administration members); and only two sock hops. At the same time the students were tired of having a run-down building, old, beat-up texts, poor laboratory facilities, an out-dated offering of German (a hold-over from the times when the neighborhood had been German), and broken windows and torn window shades. They were upset that when the school had been white there had been a junior prom and a student handbook, and that these had disappeared as the school became black. They disliked the school disciplinarian not only for her handling of students, but more particularly because she was a white woman disciplining black students. Finally, they were concerned that some of their teachers were too old, or unfair, or appeared to be prejudiced against their black students.

The small discussion group I was in took up this problem of appearing to be prejudiced. The other members of the group happened to be younger and older white women, including one who had twice been threatened by some girls in her class. Some of the women, although they thought they enjoyed excellent rapport with their students, were actually disliked behind their backs because the students thought they were prejudiced. Knowing it would be impossible to convince them that they acted in prejudicial ways toward their black students and that they thereby created a communication barrier, the group leader and I tried only to show that many students *think* their white teachers are prejudiced, and therefore react to them as though they were in fact racially prejudiced. The teachers were astounded that perhaps they didn't understand their students after all, and that their students didn't understand them. Our group leader pointed out to us how small can be the incident that provokes misunderstanding. "Students (or Class or People), open your books to page 135" opens a void between teacher and students, he explained, while "Let's open our books to page 135" creates a bond, or at least keeps from opening the void at that spot. The difference lies in the pronouns "us" and "we" instead of "you" and "I." I was surprised at that particular example, but when I stood before a group of students at the evaluation session at the end of the day and told them that we had learned at least that much, they cheered.

Not cheering, but consternation followed this revelation in the teachers' group. For even though beginning to understand the great gap that unconsciously exists between teachers and students, these women still balked at making a special effort to reach their students. Students shouldn't need special consideration, was their argument. Almost in vain the group leader and I argued that, whether or not students *should* need special consideration, these particular students *did,* and we white teachers therefore had to make a special effort to reach them. I disagreed with all those teachers, black and white, who argued that our students were just like any other students and didn't need to be treated differently just because they were black. White teachers have to take many more pains in their relations with black students, as any little injustice may rightly or wrongly be interpreted as racial discrimination. We have enough obstacles to surmount in teaching without adding racial hostility from our students to the list.

Not only were the workshops held too late in the year—May 23—to head off any of our racial problems, it was also too late by then to schedule a follow-up session. The purpose of such a day would have been to discuss any changes the administration might have made after the first day of workshops, to discover whether tensions had abated any and to see what still remained to be done to bring the faculty and students back into harmony with themselves and with each other. Since we did not have this second day at Donner, the impact of the first was necessarily lessened. Some changes were made, though. The activity fee was reduced to one dollar with no apparent diminution of activities for the next year; girls' washrooms on the third floor were unlocked (I think they had been locked because there weren't enough women teachers to check all the washrooms between periods for smoking). At the end of the school year we were told that the following fall a popular young black teacher was to become the faculty-sponsor-editor of the school newspaper, and the disciplinarian would become head of counseling.

Whether from the workshops or just because the end of the year was in sight, the atmosphere lightened. June 21, the magic last day of school, drew nearer and nearer, and I couldn't help but review the year and tote up my successes and failures.

I have the deepest sympathy for my third period seniors, an active, alert group who would have responded even better to a dynamic, well-prepared teacher than they did to me. Instead they got bits and pieces of apathy, lethargy, urban history, prohibition, smoking, drugs, and the war in Vietnam. We had a real love-hate relationship, that class and I. Because they were my brightest class, I felt most guilty about them, the mornings after my do-nothing nights. Our relationship reached a crisis in November.

For several weeks my unpreparedness and consequent guilt had been growing worse, until I was a nervous wreck before, during, and after third period each day. Each week we had fewer and fewer discussions and more and more in-class writing assignments, as I desperately attempted to keep from them the knowledge that I had nothing prepared to discuss. To a man they resented the new regimen, and the distance between us steadily grew. Boredom and restlessness were written all over their faces, sometimes erupting into mutterings in the back of the room. Restlessness is a contagious disease and was beginning to spread. Not only was I unprepared, I was paranoically sure they *knew*

I was unprepared (no doubt this is true), and came to class only to leer at me and put me on the spot.

Their chronic tardiness worsened the situation. The excuse was that their homerooms met in the auditorium two flights down and at the other end of the building, and that four minutes wasn't enough time to move that distance through crowded hallways. "Especially when you dawdle and talk along the way," I would mutter nastily to myself. I knew the way to end the tardiness was simply to shut the door when the bell rang, and begin the lesson. But what's the point when you have no lesson to begin?

The confrontation came during the second week of November, when no one but one boy, one of the three remaining white students in that class, showed up. Usually, as the bell rang, there were four or five students seated, and about ten more straggling in, but this day there wasn't a soul around. "This is it," I thought, "they've finally gone ahead and organized a boycott to protest this rotten class. I can't say as I blame them, but how am I going to face them when they return, and how am I going to explain it to the administration?"

"Where is everybody?" my one student innocently inquired— innocently, because (I think) he would have been left out of any action planned by the black students in class.

I had no answer. "But where is Pam?" my mind ran (Joanne's absence never occurred to me), realizing that she, too wasn't there, yet would never be part of a boycott if it was organized by black students. On the other hand I admitted that she might be staging a boycott of her own.

Three or four minutes passed by the time I had thought all this out and had completed several trips into the hall without spotting anyone. How was I going to get them back? Where were they? Parading in front of the principal's office, or inside talking to him?

As though by prearrangement they then began trickling in without a word of explanation or excuse. I decided to take the angry approach, hoping my hurt and wounded pride wouldn't show too much. "I've had it!" I exploded nervously, but was only three or four sentences into my harangue when several voices calmly broke in to explain that they had had class elections in homeroom and had been detained.

Yet despite this incident and all it represented, it was in this same class that we had the liveliest and most interesting discussions, on every topic that came to mind. One of my aims as their teacher was to train them to think about the world around them. I reserved at least one day a week for discussion of current events or for a current events quiz. In this class the discussions often could have continued long after our forty minutes were over. In the seventh period, on the other hand, if a discussion got going at all, it died halfway through the period.

Precisely because the seventh period seniors were such "sleepies," I have far less compassion for them even though they suffered through the same bill of fare as the third period class. As a group they never ceased being friendly, but several of them, such as Gertrude, Frank, Bruce, and our star athlete Whitney, were chronic cutters; and the brightest of the lot and the most fun— Luther, editor of the *Rocking Horse*—fell in love March 31 and was utterly useless from that day forward. These absences couldn't help but cut down on the spirit of the group.

In keeping with my determination to get my students thinking, I tried to remain impartial in front of them on current issues. On the broad spectrum of race they knew where I stood, but not until the last day of our study of Vietnam did they know I was against the war. Actually this wasn't due to successful impartiality on my part; it was really that my frequent sardonic comments went over their heads. A student surprised me into awareness of their political anonymity one afternoon late in the year. Just after I had made a particularly biased remark against the war, he asked whether I was for the war or against it. I couldn't believe my ears, so I took a vote. Only two or three in each class thought they knew where I stood, and of those few, the majority thought I was pro-war. Even Luther, more aware than most and actively anti-war, had only just realized where I stood. Understandably, after the vote each class thought I was going to tell them my views—to give them, in effect, the gospel truth about Vietnam. Should they support the war or should they fight it? Their history teacher would tell them. But I refused, and they were taken aback. My rationale, as I explained to them, was that if I told them how I felt, some of them would immediately adopt my views in the hope of getting A's, and others out of sheer perversity would automatically take the opposite view. "Even more important than that," I concluded, "if I am able to sway you just by telling you my views, then anybody could come along after me and sway you to his side. And that's not going to help any of us. Instead of my giving you some predigested opinions, you are going to have to study these articles and draw your own conclusions." Imagine, then, how happy I was to hear my one vocal anti-Communist student exclaim a couple of weeks later, "You know, reading these articles gives you an entirely different picture of the war."

Cheating wasn't a significant problem, but it did occur in all of my classes. What surprised me about it was, not its existence, but it crudity (or was it just that I discovered only the crudely-executed attempts?). Yet judging from their shock at being discovered, the students must have thought they were being remarkably clever. Two incidents stand out from all the rest.

On an essay test George had written something utterly unintelligible that I was at a loss to decipher. Later, in reading another paper, I realized what it was he had been trying to say. I knew George sat directly behind another person, so I checked back to his paper and everything fell into place: George had been copying, all right, but he had been unable to read what he was copying, so had put down groups of letters of the same approximate shapes and length, *even though his paper then made absolutely no sense!* In trying to be helpful, I circled the passage in question and wrote, "George, you need glasses. What Carl actually wrote was . . ." George didn't cheat again that I know of.

The second noteworthy incidence of cheating occurred early in November, on our first current events quiz. This one was a joint effort by Torrey and Carmine. I had decided to have the class exchange papers and grade them, to save me some work. I was careful to instruct everyone to sign his name on the bottom of the paper he was correcting, and to use pen if the test was written in pencil, and vice versa. I didn't know why I had them do such things; I only remembered that my teachers had always had us do them. That night I discovered the reasons for these precautions: Torrey and Carmine had very kindly filled in the blank spaces on each others' papers.

The following day, without mentioning names, I told the class that I had uncovered some cheating. After a few words from me on cheating and self-respect, Carmine wanted to know how I had found out. In answering her query I looked directly at her, which provoked the demand, "What are you looking at me for?

I didn't do anything!" Then one girl remarked disgustedly, "You asked the question, that's why she's looking at you." In my own sweetly perverse way I couldn't help but add, "Feeling guilty?" On both of their papers I had written "See me after class." Carmine did and denied the whole thing. Torrey didn't stop to talk—he just turned in his writing assignment of the day and fled. I didn't press the point with him just then, as he was obviously feeling bad enough about it already. What I didn't realize until that night was that he was handing in the paper reprinted below.

"Cheating, cheating is one of the most common happenings in school kids today! Why do you cheat? Well, I can't tell you why anyone else cheats! I can only tell of my own experience, when my teacher wrote on my paper see me'. This was not a good feeling to see this on my paper for believe it or not it was my first and last time cheating. And to think I got caught! But I'm glad for if I have had the opportunity, I would probally think I could get away with it again.

"Before hand I never cheated, Because it's only hurting myself, I felt you didn't cheat the teacher you were cheating yourself. As my grandmother use to say "If you cheat you'll steal and if you'll steal you'll lie.

"I didn't want to cheat. Understand me clearly now, I didn't have to cheat! I did cheat but I was influenced by others. I felt bad going home thinking about I had cheated. That's why when I got my paper I felt ashame.

"I told my little brother, I'll help him with his homework every night if he promised not to cheat.

"Cheating is unessacary for when you're out of school and you have cheated your way out you in turn will be cheated out of an education! Don't cheat! Bee sweet." (Smile)

Moral: Experience is the best Teacher.
And Knowledge is the best Leader"

Carmine didn't deny it again.

Even in cheating, the juniors are entirely different from the seniors. The juniors would whisper answers across the room (always the wrong ones); they would noticeably crane their necks to see someone else's paper; or they would actually get up, walk over, and look at it. From the laughter this latter tactic always drew, however, I think it was more a bid for attention than an attempt to cheat, although it was that too.

Another difference in the two groups, already noted, lay in their behavior. I never even got the juniors under control, let alone worry about the intellectual paucity of their classes. Theirs was an essential-level (that is, slow) world history class. We began with a study of the Renaissance, moving into the growth of trade and exploration, and from there into African slavery. And that's where we ended, in June: with slavery. (And that is why I never filled out the history department chairman's sheet on topics covered in class during the year. Too embarrassed!) For the life of me I can't figure out how we managed to waste so much time. Granted, it was noisy. Granted, they were slow students. Granted, I didn't have the slightest idea how to teach slow students. Still, I simply cannot imagine what we did those seventy or eighty days between the end of January and the end of June. Perhaps I am repressing it, but to do that there must be something to repress.

I do recall pangs of guilt over our pace, as I also recall wondering which was the better plan: to finish the course at the risk of their not understanding any of it, or to go slowly enough for them to understand some of it. I chose the latter, which the slower students told me they appreciated; but it bored the brighter ones, so I divided them into two groups. This, too, is a sin of sorts, for the division was obviously one of smarter-slower. Trying to placate the borderline cases, I pleaded innocent to the charge, claiming that in order to get the two groups of equal size I was forced to put some of the smarter students in with the talkers and trouble-makers. Actually that wasn't so far from wrong: I didn't necessarily put all slow students together, but I did put all skill-poor students together. The two groups worked from different texts and met on different days, and while I don't know that it helped any of the students, just knowing I wouldn't have to hear Salinda, "the chatterer," every day gave me a big boost. Carol still appeared, though, to ask if she had to come to class that day.

There were some good things about the class. On a questionnaire run by the MAT program, these same students who bugged me every day of the year remarked that I came across as a human being who was interested in them as individuals, who encouraged everyone to speak in class and let everyone have his say, who acknowledged the fact that they were black and she was white, and made no bones about it, and who tried to explain things so everyone could understand. This evaluation pleased me a great deal, as this was the kind of person I had tried to be. That was one good thing about my fourth period. I don't think there were any others. It's just too bad I was such an incompetent teacher of world history. But then, since we know everyone forgets the facts anyway, being a congenial and understanding human being was more important!

More important, but not enough. I knew after two or three weeks of school that my students liked me, but that was an empty victory if I didn't then go ahead and do something for them. I have always thought high school should be a time and place of preparation for adult life. Specifically, graduating seniors should leave knowing something of the world around them and having the tools for learning more and for handling whatever tasks they might face. If they are headed for college, they shouldn't have to fail from a lack of basic skills. If going directly to work, they should have the rudimentary skills that would enable them to hold and grow into a specific job. Skills that are common to every aspect of successful adult life are reading and writing. Without competence in these two areas one's job capabilities are severely limited, usually to the service industries and factory work.

Every year high schools graduate thousands of students equipped only for these two job areas, that is, for jobs with low wages and little job security or opportunity for advancement. This fact has nothing to do with the intelligence of the people involved, only with the fact that they can't read or write well enough to qualify for more challenging work. Tracing the problem to its origins, statistics show that it is way back in third and fourth grades that these students begin falling behind the national norms in reading and writing, a failing that handicaps them throughout the rest of their school career and, by limiting their job and higher education opportunities, follows them throughout their adult life. Torrey is a case in point. Having taken a business math course in high school, his office skills are probably adequate to enable him to land a job. And though he has an engaging personality and wants to be an accountant, his grammar and spelling will hold him back from ever being any more than a clerk in an office pool, a job that will draw on his office skills, but never challenge or interest him for any length of time. Many of my seniors went on to college. I can't help wondering how many will make it through freshman year English, let alone any other course which requires a good deal of reading and reading comprehension.

I opened this chapter by stating that I don't want to teach high school again. The minus quality of my teaching, with which I have dealt extensively in this chapter, really has little to do with it. Almost all first-year teachers are sorely disappointed in themselves, and what they lack in competence they make up in youth and freshness, which is at least as important from the students' point of view. Here, then, is the real reason for not wanting to return to a high school classroom: it's too discouraging. So I was a Human Being. So my contemporary history classes were more interesting than other teachers' because we examined current issues and had free and open discussions. So what? If I didn't manage at the same time to improve the prospects for a better adult life that they had when they entered my class in September, then I didn't do enough. Many of us wasted a great deal of time and energy arguing the merits of Black culture and language versus White middle-class culture and language and whether we should impose the latter on our students. We thought we were so radical! There is no reason to exclude all but White middle-class norms from the classroom, as is currently practiced, and to devalue Black culture and language, or lower-class White, as the case may be. But we must at the same time continue to teach, and make certain our students acquire competence in mainstream society's language and culture in order that they may choose their job and their way of life and not be forced into one culture and out of the other through a lack of familiarity with both. This says nothing about the merits of one culture over another. It only says that schools must not, by default or otherwise, decide their students' futures for them. Even if we think midstream American society is the most amoral and valueless culture in history, we must allow our students to choose for themselves whether or not they want to enter it. This means, in the first instance, enabling everyone to get a good education; that is, making sure everyone learns to read and write so that they may take advantage of the education offered them. Reading and writing are hardly the only problems in our society, and schools and school teachers are hardly the only ones to blame for illiteracy; but the responsibility for correcting the situation does lie with the public schools.

When I say my desire not to teach high school again has everything to do with the students I taught, I mean I liked them too well not to be discouraged over their probable futures. Yet it has nothing to do with those particular students because the problem is city- and nation-wide, and I could have encountered it in any one of a thousand high schools, white or black, anywhere in the country.

The logical extension of this line of thought is that I should become a primary school reading teacher. I didn't arrive at this conclusion while school was still in session, however. In fact, after the May 23 human relations workshops, time seemed to telescope, and I had no opportunity for serious thought. After all, my fiancé had returned to Chicago; we were busy planning the wedding; and I was still teaching school—at least, I was still going to school every day. During the last three weeks of school, painters, desk-sanders, and wall-washers descended en masse and robbed us of our classrooms for several days at a time. Initially I tried to hold classes in the auditorium for my two senior classes, but these were graduating seniors and June was their month to stand around looking important. On June 11, ten days before the end of school, the seniors received their grades and never returned to class, even though officially they were due there for three more days. With the wedding planned for just one week after school closed, I had plenty to do at home, so I didn't mind the disruptions in my teaching routine. In fact, losing the seniors left me with just homeroom and one class to teach, so from then on I sneaked out after fourth period, two hours after I had arrived.

By the time the last day of school arrived I was so enveloped in wedding plans that I had no time to savor it. In effect I was robbed of feeling any relief at the end to the hardships of the past ten months. Even now, the poignancy of those hardships is beginning to fade. Perhaps I am secretly relieved not to be teaching in the fall (I'm taking a year off). By a year from September, however, if I am not back in school to become a primary reading teacher, I *may* be ready and—*perhaps*—anxious to face the challenge of another year of teaching.

Kevin Ryan

The First Year of Teaching

Teaching is a noble profession. Regrettably, the nobility of the calling does not insure the nobility of the teacher. People become teachers for a variety of reasons and to fulfill a variety of conscious and unconscious needs. Some teach because they have been excited by knowledge that they wish to pass on to others. Others because they feel that it is the only thing for which college has prepared them, or because they hated their high school education and want to make things different. Some teach because they want an "insurance policy" against the future, because teaching is a socially acceptable way to spend the time between graduation from college and marriage, or because it is a stepping stone to administration or other careers in education. And there are those who teach because they have a passion to shape the lives of others. Undoubtedly, many who casually enter teaching become fascinated by its challenges and its rewards, while others for whom teaching is the fulfillment of childhood dreams, find nothing but disappointment.

While most young teachers enter the schools with fervor and dedication, generally the beginner's commitment to teaching as a long-term career is not high. Evidence for this is the teacher drop-out rate during the first year. Over fifty percent of those who receive certification upon graduation are not teaching two years later.[1] Over half of the first-year teachers do not intend to

1. R. N. Bush, "The Formative Years," in *The Real World of the Beginning Teacher* (Washington, D.C.: National Commission on Teacher Education and Professional Standards, National Education Association, 1965), p. 7.

be teaching five years later.[2] The low salaries and low social status of teachers are frequently cited as causes for lack of commitment and the high drop-out rate. This may very well be an over-simplification, since many young people today are more concerned with job satisfaction than with social status. For many, too, a career in teaching represents upward social mobility. In addition, starting salaries have been improving rapidly. For instance, in Chicago a first-year teacher with a B.A. receives $8,220 for ten months employment.

Another reason for the low level of commitment to the profession may be that teaching suffers from overfamiliarity. For the young person choosing a career, teaching appears to hold no mystery. It is a known quantity. If a career glamour poll were taken, it would probably stand quite far down on the list, perhaps between bank telling and waiting on tables. Too often it is as hard to work up a commitment to teaching as it is to drum up a romance with the girl next door.

College professors, who are important people to future teachers, often do not help the situation. Few academicians encourage their ablest students to enter precollegiate teaching. Although they are among the first to condemn the performance of the American schools, they are among the last to encourage their finest students to enter high school teaching. The young scholar is guided into graduate programs in the disciplines, but not in education. He soon gets the impression from his mentor that if he is going to serve, he should take the high road—an academic program leading to college teaching and a professorship.

Robert Bush of Stanford University, however, would not let the blame lie long at the door of academics. Bush writes candidly of the school of education's lax efforts as gatekeeper to the profession.

> Our response to the knock is, I'm afraid, an added problem. It is often too glib, too readily affirmative. Standards for admission vary so widely that almost anyone with a little patience, if he inquires at a few places, can be admitted to training for a career in teaching. Too often the candidate's application is not treated in a thoughtful or business-like manner. Regular

2. Ward S. Mason, *The Beginning Teacher: A Survey of New Teachers in Public Schools, 1956–57* (Washington, D.C.: United States Government Printing Office, 1958).

standards are lacking. The procedure may be so informal as to verge on being lackadaisical, or when it is formalized, it may be wooden, mechanical, or almost perfunctory.[3]

The low standards implicit in these procedures are common knowledge among the profession's recruitment sources, the college students. Few young men are overly proud that they qualify for the armed forces. So, too, few can get very excited about being eligible to teach.

All of these—the mixed motives of the beginning teachers, a high drop-out rate, and low commitment—work against the interest of the individual first-year teacher. Administrators and senior teachers often are too busy to take the new teacher very seriously. Since he will probably be with them a short time, they expend very little extra energy on him and hope he does a good job. The beginning teacher, then, finds it difficult to feel special or important. He does not see the community as supportive or as interested in him. The taxpayer resists higher salaries, better working conditions, and especially more money spent on in-service training. And it is these very factors which perpetuate low standards and weak commitment.

How They Learn to Teach

The cliché "teachers are born, not made" is a useless slogan that has trapped generations of educators into meaningless argument. It runs contrary to all we know about human growth and development. However, its existence does highlight the confusion about just how teachers learn to teach. Although a precise description of how teachers learn to teach is lacking, there appear to be at least four categories of resources which beginners draw on as they learn their profession. The four categories are sequential: first, our human tendencies to teach others; second, the example of former teachers; third, formal education courses and student teaching; and, fourth, the actual experience of the first year in a classroom.

The human race has survived because we have taught one another. As a result, people have built-in tendencies to teach, tendencies which have evolved over the long history of the race. As J. M. Stephens has pointed out,

3. Bush, "The Formative Years," p. 3.

Some of these non-deliberated, spontaneous tendencies are: first, to speak of what we know; second, to react to the behavior of others; third, to point to the moral; and fourth, to supply the answer that temporarily eludes the other fellow.[4]

These "let-me-tell-you" and "I-told-you-so" tendencies are deeply ingrained in the beginning teacher, as they are in all people. While these tendencies may be very helpful for primitive teaching situations, they may indeed inhibit the classroom learning of children. One would guess, for instance, that it is more important for a teacher to be able to ask a good question than to provide students with an answer. It is more important for the teacher to encourage the pursuit of knowledge than to bring the pursuit to a close. It may be, therefore, that these built-in teaching tendencies hinder the beginner in becoming an effective teacher.

Teacher-watching is a second type of resource beginners draw upon. The prospective teacher has been watching his own teachers for sixteen or seventeen years. During that time he has made judgments about certain teaching practices of which he approves or disapproves. He has consciously and unconsciously identified certain techniques, methods, and attitudes that he likes and hopes to emulate. Also, every young teacher has acquired over the years at least one former teacher after whom he hopes to model his teaching. Such a rich background of vicarious experience can be a valuable asset. However, this familiarity with the teacher's role has some drawbacks. As Dan Lortie has suggested, "The flow of influence from one generation to another may account for the conservatism of the schools."[5] The methods and techniques the beginner copies from his former teachers may have been learned by those teachers thirty or forty years ago. In fact, these same teaching practices may have been copies made by the "model teachers" from their own former teachers. Unfortunately, the test of time does not insure relevance to today's classrooms.

There is another more pressing problem inherent in modeling oneself after another teacher. The teaching practices that appealed to the beginning teacher when he was a student may not work with his students. One person may have thrived under the

4. J. M. Stephens, "Research in the Preparation of Teachers: Background Factors That Must Be Considered," unpublished paper delivered at the Ontario Institute for the Study of Education, April 1968, p. 3.
5. Dan C. Lortie, "Teacher Socialization: The Robinson Crusoe Model," in *The Real World Of the Beginning Teacher*, p. 59.

tutelage of a strict and authoritarian teacher, but he may fail completely when he tries to assume this style as a teacher. Or, more likely, he may wish to be extremely permissive and find himself incapable of pulling it off. Finally, many beginning teachers burden themselves with unrealistic expectations. In trying to model themselves after their ideal teacher, they may be stacking the cards against the development of their own natural talents and strengths. Linda Corman was well into her first year before she realized she could not imitate the styles of her favorite teachers. She needed to learn this painful lesson before she could begin to develop her own style.

Professional education courses and experiences are a third means by which teachers learn how to teach. This category contains the formal and official sources of teacher training. It includes everything from the introductory course in education to student teaching. The much maligned education courses have been a focus of controversy for years. Beginning teachers usually complain that they are too theoretical and have little relevance to classroom practices. They also complain that their professors of education are too far removed from the daily give-and-take of the classroom. Perhaps the new muscular voice of college students will be instrumental in bringing about change. The recent response to the problem is to cut down the number of education courses. While this may be a good in itself, alone this does not ease the beginning teacher's entrance into the schools.

The antagonism toward education courses is misdirected. Instead of simply fewer education courses, what may indeed be needed are more experiences which help the student put theory into practice and acquire the skills and strategies of good teaching. Much of the ire behind the complaints stems from the beginning teacher's inability to turn his education courses into a survival kit for the classroom. Many beginners try to practice such educational ideals as student-directed discussions and small-group instruction, but fail, becoming embittered about "the impractical theory we were fed back at the Ivory Tower." Since the schools are filled with teachers who have not lived up to the ideals they acquired in the university, the beginning teacher receives reinforcement for his hostile attitudes among his new peers. The problem is simply that telling someone a theory does not insure that he has the complex behavior patterns necessary to make it work in a classroom.

Student teaching is consistently rated by teachers as the most valuable of the formal components of professional education. Although some professional educators like to think of it as the qualifying test for beginners, so few students fail at it that this assertion looks rather foolish. If it is a test at all, student teaching is a self-test for the prospective teacher by which he decides whether or not he likes teaching. And in this regard it provides valuable information, although it comes rather late in training to aid in career planning.

Student teaching suffers from the same malady as education courses. Too much is expected of it. It is unreasonable to expect that student teaching can accomplish the awesome task of preparing a neophyte for full teaching responsibility in ten weeks. Even under the best of conditions, the experience is too short and has too many built-in limitations to do the entire job of preparation. Further, there are too few master teachers by whom the beginners can be guided. Nevertheless, student teaching is still rated as the most relevant aspect of teacher education.

The experience of the first year is a fourth resource by which teachers learn to teach. "There is no substitute for experience" is a favorite axiom of teachers. One day in early September, the hopeful beginner is given responsibility for certain classes—and the test is on. The first year of teaching is a confrontation. The beginner must act, must respond. Out of the new teacher's need to act comes a great hurly-burly of activity, some effective and some not. He assigns homework and discovers that it is much more than students can handle. He gropes to find the suitable amount. He plans a lesson in the evening; the following day he discovers that his plan only takes fifteen minutes, and he has nothing for the students to do for the rest of the hour. Another day he plans a lesson, and he discovers that he has actually packed enough material in the lesson to keep the class busy for a week. All of this is part of the important learning of the first year of teaching.

Lortie has compared attempts to gain mastery in the classroom with Robinson Crusoe's fight for survival:

The beginning teacher may find that prior experience supplies him with some alternatives for action, but his crucial learning comes from his personal errors; he fits together special solutions and specific problems into some kind of whole and at times finds leeway for the expression of personal taste. Working largely alone, he cannot make the specifics of his working knowledge base explicit, nor need he, as his victories are private.[6]

Much of the first year's experience-based learning is gleaned from the trial-and-error method. This is a hard way to learn, hard on both the teacher and the students. Also, trial-and-error learning does not insure that the beginning teacher is actually learning things which make him a better teacher. One person's first-year experience may teach him how to dominate students so that they fear him and do exactly what he asks. Another beginner may learn how to combine all his talents to become a superior teacher. The six beginners in this book tell stories of searching and testing. They are forced to thrust aside their dreams and fantasies about the kind of teachers they were going to be as they grope for ways to survive. Idealism gives way to pragmatism as they seek answers to very pressing questions: How can I motivate Paul? How can I keep my freshmen under control? Why is there no life in that third-period class? How can I get through to my students? How should I react to this situation? To that situation? *What works?*

The beginning teacher, then, has four resources from which he learns to teach. All are different. All may provide him with a different understanding of what teaching is. None of these sources is without serious limitations. While some of our greatest teachers have learned in this way, so too have some of our worst. It is difficult to have confidence in a teacher training system which has had such uneven results.

The Shock of the Familiar

The first year of teaching is a patchwork of the known and the unknown, the anticipated and the unanticipated, the familiar and the unfamiliar. Although this could be said about any occupation, its effect is heightened for the beginning teacher. Young lawyers and social workers, for example, enter professions about which they have little solid knowledge. Their views of the daily life they will be taking on is frequently stereotyped and highly

6. Ibid.

romanticized. The reasons are obvious. There has been little opportunity for the young lawyer or social worker to carefully study the role which he has chosen. He may, indeed, have gathered a great deal of professional information, but his moment-by-moment work and the stuff of his daily existence as a lawyer or social worker is unavailable until he begins.

The beginning teacher, on the other hand, thinks he knows what he is getting into. The daily life of a teacher holds few secrets for him. He is no stranger to the school. He has been there before. The beginning teacher, unlike all other professionals, has had opportunities to observe closely the occupants of the role to which he aspires. By the time he has graduated from high school he has spent over 16,000 hours in school. This is equivalent in time to having seen 10,000 movies! More than he realizes, the ebb and flow of life in the school is in his marrow.

By the time the first-year teacher enters his own classroom, he has been exposed at very close range to between fifty and seventy teachers. These figures do not take into account the teachers he has watched and studied as part of his pre-service observation program. For seventeen years he has sat under the gaze of teachers and scrutinized them in return. His teachers' ability to control the class, their fairness, their humor, their dress—all were noted and analyzed. Teachers were the frequent source of discussions. No idiosyncrasy went undetected. No social virtue or personal defect was above discussion. It often seems that students spend more time studying the teacher than the course.

The school routine of classes, homeroom, study halls, clubs, sports, and exams is well known to the beginning teacher. He knows about the student subculture patterns of in-groups and out-groups, and of cliques and outcasts, even though the forms and fashions have shifted somewhat. The existence of ceremonies and pageantry surrounding such events as a big game and an honor-society induction is taken for granted. For most, then, the rituals and routines of the high school do not have to be learned. The beginning teacher has been part of all this. He has lived through it. Still, the first year of teaching is a shock.

The shock comes when the beginner changes from audience to actor. The role which he had seen played out thousands of times is now his. The familiar scene of the classroom is reversed, and he encounters a startling new situation. Wylie Crawford ruefully opens his account by pointing out that in September a favorite theory of his had been that "teaching was simply the other side of the coin from studying." What he discovered as he groped with the role of teacher is that he had never fully understood it.

The shock of the first year of teaching is difficult to discuss because each beginner's experience is unique. It is a product of the interaction of his own psyche and the milieu of his school. Amid the familiar surroundings of classrooms and students loom events and individuals for which the beginner is unprepared. Young teachers report a variety of causes for their shock. They find high school students are hard to reach; they underestimate the difficulty of motivating them and overestimate their own skills as disciplinarians. They do not anticipate the amount of time and work necessary to keep up with students. The volume of administrative tasks surprises them. They are unprepared to handle classes *and* take roll, write tardy slips, read notices from the office, and execute the dozens of ever-present administrative details. The emotional and physical drain of teaching five periods a day leaves them little energy for anything else. They are hurt by unprovoked hostility from their students. The invisible barriers which keep their students from understanding concepts and ideas stagger them. They are crushed by the students' disdain for the subject matter they so cherish. Some are overwhelmed by the discovery that they do not like adolescents. Some, like Linda Corman, don't like what they see themselves become as a result of the teaching experience. Others, like John Canfield, are disappointed by many of their colleagues; they come expecting a community of scholars and find ordinary people toiling at the job.

Of course, the first year of teaching is not always unpleasant. Some beginners are tremendously relieved to discover that their fantasies of failure do not come true. They are surprised to find out that they can teach, that they like what they are doing, and that students do respect them. For some, anticipated sources of trouble turn out to be their strengths: they *do* have good command of their subject matter; they *can* be fair to all the students and avoid playing favorites. For some, teaching is their very first job, and they get a tremendous satisfaction out of finally being autonomous adults, being treated like adults, and *even* getting paid for it. But whether the first year of teaching is a sad one or a joyous one, it is a year of intense learning for all.

What Teachers Learn during Their First Year

There is pain and pleasure in learning. Confrontation with what we do not know can hurt. Struggling with the unknown can be uncomfortable. But there is also the satisfaction of mastery, of being able to do something which before had eluded us. So it is with learning to teach.

As the six accounts make clear, there is much to learn during the first year of teaching. One of the most surprising things a first-year teacher learns is that his official role in the classroom does not permit him the luxury of being himself. Something about the institutionalized nature of the secondary school inhibits the young teacher from being himself. The obvious inhibitors are his students. Students want to encounter a "teacher" because they have learned how to coexist with teachers. An idiosyncratic and unpredictable "person" puts them off. They don't know how to deal with him. When students deal with teachers, they are on famil-, iar ground; there are certain ritualistic behaviors which both go through. There is a clearly identified social distance between students and teacher. Neither is allowed to get too close to the other. There are certain subjects they don't talk about. Vocabularies are restricted. The first name which Wylie Crawford lamented losing was lost to the system and its rituals. Although teachers become extremely fond of some of their students and develop intense dislikes for others, they simply cannot give in to those feelings. Nor can students freely express their affection or distaste for teachers.

Since the unwritten rules of the classroom forbid the young teacher from being himself, he must struggle to find a suitable mask, a suitable *persona*. We see this vividly in the accounts by Cornog, Corman, and Crawford. When they tried to be natural, students rejected them; therefore, they were forced to become actors. Much of their first year was devoted to experimenting and awkwardly testing out different parts. Like T. S. Eliot's J. Alfred Prufrock, each seems to have spent his year hesitating at classroom doors "to prepare a face to meet the faces that you meet."

With the failure of each new face, the beginning teacher is persuaded to test out the role of that old standard: the authoritarian, aloof teacher. This role is usually successful for him because it is the role the students expect. Further, it is the role he has encountered most frequently during his own schooling. While most teachers at one time or another are forced into this role, some in subsequent years are secure enough to let the mask drop occasionally and to reveal their essential humanity. Most experienced teachers learn to slip in and out of this part with ease. As they enter the school building in the morning, the mask is put on, and it remains on all day, only to be removed for a short period in the faculty room.

The first year of teaching can be an emotional roller coaster during which the beginning teacher learns a good deal about his emotional makeup. There is a quality of being carried along by the force of one's newly tapped emotions. The rude remark of a student can call up a red anger that the beginner never knew he possessed. His own cutting remark to a student can momentarily bring a cruel sense of triumph and, later, unaccustomed shame. His inability to get a student interested in a particular lesson can generate an unfamiliar frustration. Many situations, which he will learn to live with later, take on a special significance in this initial stage. As a beginner he is *vulnerable*. He is trying to prove to himself, to his students, and to his superiors that he is a teacher. Any evidence which either supports or weakens this contention triggers a strong emotional response.

A veteran teacher, experienced in supervising beginning teachers, summarized one of their major difficulties: "They think their students are just like them, only smaller." The first-year secondary school teacher is usually amazed at how much he has forgotten about high school students in four or five years. Much of the first year is spent in rediscovering the nature of high school students and in acquiring the intangible but all important sense of the teaching-learning process.

There is so much to learn. The beginning teacher must determine what his students know and what they do not know. What are realistic expectations for them? How much can they do? What is the proper vocabulary for different levels of students? To what type of humor are they responsive?

The new teacher must also learn how to organize ideas and at the same time deal with the dynamics of thirty students. He must be able to listen and at the same time anticipate the next question. And he must learn to check the students' understanding.

The beginning teacher must develop a good pace for his instruction. He must be able to tell when the students need variety and when they have had enough instruction to work productively on their own.

Another skill that must be developed is the knack of interesting students in a particular task. What kinds of students respond to different kinds of material? What are the best sources for interesting material in his field?

Finally, the new teacher must learn to budget time. How much time should be spent on preparation? How much on paper grading? How can "administrivia" be dispensed with quickly but efficiently?

There are no hard-and-fast answers to these questions. At present, each teacher has to get the feel for these matters for himself, and on the job.

Many unpleasant aspects of teaching never appear in education texts or courses. It is rarely pointed out, for instance, that high school students can be extremely cruel to one another and that frequently they are cruel to their teachers. Students like Gary Cornog's Brian are not rarities, but somehow they escape mention. It is not uncommon for docile classes to become transformed into packs intent upon bringing the teacher to bay. We all have heard quite civilized college students and adults recount with smiles and obvious relish how their high school class caused poor Miss Dimppy to have a nervous breakdown or how they drove that young math teacher so wild that he finally quit at mid-year. There is a tendency of educators to describe high school students as they would like them to be rather than as they are. This unrealistic view takes its toll. Studies of teachers' attitudes toward children, based on the widely used Minnesota Teacher Attitude Inventory, show a sharp decline in positive attitudes toward children during the first year of teaching.[7] During the undergraduate years these attitudes had become increasingly positive. But now the beginner must stop reading and talking about children, and instead must deal with them as they are—warts and all.

Nor is the young teacher told about the continual uncertainty of that first year, when he will not yet have learned to predict the behavior of students, or of himself. There is also the existential terror of being asked a question one should really know, and

7. J. W. Getzels and P. W. Jackson, "The Teacher's Personality and Characteristics," in *Handbook of Research on Teaching,* ed. Nathan Gage (Chicago: Rand McNally, 1963), p. 509.

being unable to answer it. (In education courses you are told to admit to the students that you don't know, but when you try that and see the smirks on their faces, you begin to doubt the wisdom of this advice.) Then there is the awful embarrassment of being corrected by a student, and the terrible moment (particularly for young women) when one realizes that something she has just said has a very sexy double meaning and she sees the lewd smiles breaking out on their faces.

Few beginners are told the truth about administrators. No one admits that the principal in the modern high school cannot be an instruction leader of the faculty and that, instead, he must spend all his energy keeping the school operating from one day to the next. No one tells the new teacher that, although the principal may indeed hope that the beginner is opening up new intellectual vistas for the students, his primary concern is that the beginner cooperate with him in keeping the school running.

No one talks about how little time is spent in actually providing students with new knowledge and skills, or how much time is spent in administrative and organizational details and just plain treading water. The greatest percentage of a teacher's day is spent in nonteaching duties, if we define teaching as consciously working with children to develop knowledge and skills. Besides the out-of-class activities, like lesson planning and paper correcting, the teacher has a myriad of chores to do. He must maintain reasonable classroom behavior standards. He must check and report attendance. He must correct and hand back papers. He must act as general recorder and bookkeeper for the class. He must continually explain assignments and procedures to students. He is a source of information to the administrative staff and counselors. Frequently it seems that teaching is what he does when all the necessary activities are out of the way—a vocation to be pursued in his spare time.

The dearth of open discussion about these issues during preservice training explains why experienced teachers snicker about their alma mater being the Ivory Tower. It is difficult to understand why there is so much perverse positive thinking and sentimentality in teacher education programs. Without gossip, sports, and the students to talk about, faculty rooms would be silent. Perhaps the reason that the dark side of the teacher's daily existence never gets talked about is that we have little tolerance for the unpleasant. Also, the people who teach beginners and write books for them are usually more concerned with *what can be* or *should be* than with *what is*. Many of them, moreover, have been out of the classroom long enough for the unpleasant side of teaching to fade in prominence. Most people find it easier to remember successes and triumphs.

When the first-year teacher is surprised and unprepared for the problems he encounters, it weakens his faith in his mentors. The failure of teacher educators to deal openly with the underside of teaching has fostered education's own credibility gap. It casts a shadow on all he has been told by his education instructors. Not infrequently this failure to "tell it like it is" fosters a deep bitterness toward professional education.

Discipline: The Great Unmentionable

Nothing absorbs the energies of the first-year teacher as does lack of discipline or, as we euphemistically put it, a breakdown of classroom management. It causes depressing self-doubts, even nightmares. It leads many to abandon teaching. But for some reason, the issue of discipline remains the great unmentionable of teacher training.

Inability to maintain discipline or classroom control is the most serious contributor to teacher failure. High school students report that discipline is the major weakness of first-year teachers,[8] and certainly it is a major concern of administrators and supervisors. The accounts of the six first-year teachers are replete with troubling situations and anguish over discipline. The major recurring problem in their accounts is their attempt to get their classes under control to the point where they can teach.

We know very little about the subject of discipline and hence have little of value to say to teachers about it. This is disturbing, since discipline is so fundamental to survival and success in school. Perhaps the difficulty arises from its being such a complex phenomenon. In fact, we do not even have a good word for it. "Discipline," "classroom control," or "classroom management" are all inadequate. Although it would be hard to tell from

8. Roy C. Bryant, *Why High School Teachers Use Image Reports* (Michigan: Student Reaction Center, Western Michigan University, 1966), p. 20.

education textbooks, "discipline" is the most popular of the three
terms among teachers and students. Teachers speak of another
teacher as having "good discipline," usually meaning that the
teacher has a quality which affects students in such a way that
they maintain generally acceptable standards of behavior and
respect.

Discipline has little to do with teaching per se, except that it
is a necessary condition for teaching to take place. It is the *sine
qua non*. As is evident from the previous accounts, the discipline
problem is also a matter of degree and kind. There are the kinds
of situations which Eleanor Fuke encountered on her first day
of teaching, when she walked into a class that was a vortex of
running, yelling students. At the other extreme are situations like
those which Gary Cornog describes so sensitively, when the students give the teacher very subtle cues that they think he is a
"nut." Here the issue is one of respect. It is taxing, indeed, for
the teacher to concentrate on his lesson if his students are showing him that they find him silly, laughable, irrelevant, or hateful.

Discipline problems seem to belong to the beginning teacher
in the way that pimples belong to the teen-ager. They occasionally crop up with more experienced teachers, but are generally
of minor consequence. Something there is about a beginning
teacher which makes him prey to this malady. He seems to give
off a scent of vulnerability, an odor to which his students are
keenly sensitive. Or perhaps it is an uncertainty in the eyes, or
a catch in the voice, or a slowness to respond to a student's
beyond-the-border remark. Whatever the signs, they are rarely
missed by the watchful students.

Each fall the hunting season opens in the American high school.
Like skillful gamesmen, students do not pursue their teachers during the first few weeks. They hang back and study their enemy.
The experienced teacher is not fooled by this quiescent period.
He knows he is being cased and he gives off his own subtle cues
to the effect, "If you try to bring me to bay, I'll take several of
you with me." But, alas, the beginner is not so wise. He does not
want to believe that such sinister intentions lie beneath those fresh
and innocent faces. He wants to believe that the students have
taken his measure and have found in him all they had hoped for
in a teacher. He has been lulled into a false security and has relaxed his initial intention to be firm. He has, in short, dropped his

guard, and at this point he is all but bagged. As Wylie Crawford later reflected, "The testing period was all over, and they had won."

Once the new teacher has been quietly cased, the probing stage begins. The stalkers test for soft spots. Having learned the habits of their prey, the campaign begins in earnest. If the teacher is to survive, he must respond. There is no pacifism in the classroom. Although he may not achieve victory, the beginning teacher must not lose. At stake in the battle is the loss of face—and the loss of discipline. In the high school classroom the teacher is both out-manned and out-muscled. While there may be long traditions of respect and available sources of authority, the beginner rarely knows how to call them into play. His own belief that he can do the job stands between himself and chaos.

The realization that there is a stratum of conflict just below the smooth surface of the classroom becomes apparent to most beginning teachers within the first few months. However, this knowledge does not automatically equip them with the skills with which to do battle. For many beginning teachers a large part of their time and energy during the first year is spent in fighting a rearguard action with their students. They make mistakes in the early weeks that the elephantine memories of their students will not forget. In a gentler time when the Los Angeles Dodgers were the Flatbush Bums, each fall a wail came forth from the loyal Brooklyn fans: "Wait'll next year!" This same plaintive cry is the common resolve of the first-year teacher as he plans his discipline strategy for his second year of teaching. "Wait'll next year!"

Perhaps the comparison of teen-agers to hunters stalking a victim is unfair. It is hardly the entire story of life in the high school classroom. Nor should it be inferred that this hunting phenomenon is a conscious process. Students rarely gather together and plan a "get-the-teacher" campaign. The hunt is much more instinctual. It arises from the fundamentally artifical nature of the classroom teaching-learning process. The classroom is not a natural social setting. Students do not come to class because they really want to, but because society makes demands, in many forms, that they be there. Students have no choice about who their teacher will be or who their classmates will be. They have little to say about what they are studying. They have virtually no voice in determining the procedures or ground rules of the class. Also, many are profoundly bored and are seeking ways to find excitement. It is little wonder, then, that students occasionally react to this artificial society in antisocial ways.

When students test their teachers, they are not consciously looking for weakness. They are also looking for strength. Students seek strength in their teachers—strength of personality and strength of character. They want to respect their teachers, and much of the cruelty of the hunt is due to their disappointment in finding weakness where they hoped to find human excellence. Under the guise of learning French and geometry, students are trying to learn how to become good adults. They are seeking models on which to pattern their lives. Part of being an adolescent is being uncertain, being unsure, being confused. This condition is what they hope to grow away from. So, in the fall, when they encounter a new teacher, they are looking for someone to help them. When instead they find someone who is uncertain, unsure, and a little confused, they react with disappointment and occasionally with contempt. It is a rare beginner who teaches effectively and with confidence during the initial months. Most lack the skills and the necessary *feel* for students. These deficiencies are made worse by a consciousness of their problem. Further, for many teachers this condition is compounded by their reluctance to assume the role of disciplinarian. Wylie Crawford's account graphically details how he ignored the small infractions of the students during the early weeks and how the disturbances soon multiplied and the infractions became more disruptive.

While some beginning teachers thrive on the exercise of authority, many beginners do not see the necessity of assuming classroom leadership. What is more, they do not want to. They don't want to be authority figures. They don't want to impose themselves on their students. They don't want to be feared. They wish to rule by love and sweet reason. They want a free, honest relationship with their students. They are ready to respect their students' rights and dignity, and they expect their students to respect theirs. They don't want their relationship with students to be based on preexisting codes of behavior between students and teachers. They chose teaching because they wanted to be recognized as human beings. They don't want to be like the aloof, formal, cold teachers they remember from high school. However, their students don't know this—and some wouldn't care.

Not only do beginning teachers not want to confront students about their misbehavior, but many don't know how. Before being thrust into their own classrooms, few beginning teachers have had opportunities to lead a group of adolescents. Few have ever given a command. Some have never even been in a position where they have had to ask or tell others to do things. This lack of leadership experience is particularly evident in young women. Most middle-class young women are trained to be feminine and submissive. They are trained to get their way through indirect methods (like Gary Cornog's coquettish student), rather than through direct confrontation. Most are repelled by the thought of having to tell a sixteen-year-old to "keep quiet!" And, by and large, they do not know how to do it. Nor do they know how to handle disrespect, dishonesty, or hostility. The incident between Linda Corman and the Negro girl who mocked her is certainly an unusual one. As she admits, however, the incident escalated because of her inability to handle smoothly the lesser infractions. She entangled herself in a situation which demanded the training of a top sergeant. Her frantic efforts to establish control left her open for more serious attacks. Escalation both in small wars and in handling discipline problems has proven to be a dangerous course.

In the first year of teaching, then, we witness the sad counterposing of two sets of attitudes on how the teacher should act. The students are looking for strong personalities and leadership. The beginning teacher, however, seeks a more gentle leadership style. For some few teachers, this works. For the legions, it fails. Gary Cornog wrote that he would lead forth his students out of the cave and into the clear light of truth. His self-satire reflects a new awareness that a more forceful approach is needed. It is disappointing to learn that reason is not enough, but it is a lesson teachers learn. Much of the first year is devoted to this problem. What many beginners refer to as their "idealism" in September has been tempered or readjusted by June. They are a little disappointed in themselves and a little disappointed in their students. Wisdom has been gained with the loss of innocence.

Conflicts

The first-year teacher is caught in crosscurrents of conflict. He finds himself immersed in a new and different role and in a complex social milieu. He interacts with approximately 150 students and teachers each day. In the serious, task-oriented setting of a high school, the potential for conflict is great. Young people just out of the warm, supportive atmosphere of college rarely come to the schools ready to deal with conflicts. They lack the experience and the strategies to handle these collisions. As a result, much of the first year is spent struggling with internal and external conflicts.

Not all conflict is bad. The teacher can learn much through this means. Some conflict leads to conscious decisions, such as a specific policy about dealing with children. On the other hand, the unconscious struggle to resolve classroom conflicts may have more subtle effects. For example, to avoid further hostility from an annoying, know-it-all child, the teacher may simply ignore him. To relieve the inner tension caused by knowing his teaching is putting his students to sleep, the teacher may unintentionally adopt the attitude that his students are lazy.

The abrupt transition from being a university student to being a faculty member can contribute to the beginning teacher's conflicts. In a few short months, the new teacher has gone from the high status of upper classman on the campus to the relatively low status position of novice teacher. The year before he was part of the easy social life of the campus. Now he must assume the ritualistic patterns of a high school teacher. He has gone from an environment with which he is familiar and in which he has succeeded to a largely unknown environment. He is moved from the immense personal freedom of student life to the restrictions and attendant responsibilities of professional life. As student he was concerned with abstract principles; now as teacher he must deal with concrete situations. Once he could be a passive learner; now he must be an active instructor. From being surrounded with friends and companions, he enters the isolation of a professional life. He moves from a liberal environment to a conservative one.[9] Once a client and occasional critic of the institution, he is now an employee and representative of the institution.

His values frequently lead the beginning teacher into trouble. While some would assert that the public schools belong to students and teachers, in fact they belong to the people. They are

9. W. W. Charters, "The Social Background of Teaching," in *Handbook of Research on Teaching,* p. 752.

society's mechanism to transmit the culture to the young. An important part of any culture is what the people believe in and what they hold dear—these are its values. The local school, then, is the institution in which the local society's values are reflected and taught. Since they are hired to fulfill the mission of the school, teachers are expected to reflect and teach those values. This system works well, except in a time when a culture and its values are in transition. At present we are in such times. American culture is undergoing a wrenching transformation, producing many dysfunctions and conflicts.

George Spindler, the anthropologist, has described what is happening to our society as a shift from traditional values to emergent values. He sees the traditional American values as a cluster including respect for thrift and self-denial, belief in hard work as a means to success, faith in the sacredness of the individual rather than the group, and a concern for the future rather than the present. The emergent values towards which we seem to be shifting form another cluster which includes sociability and getting along with others; a more relativistic moral attitude, which rejects absolutes; a hedonistic, present-time orientation; and an other-directed concern for group harmony.[10]

The shift in values has not been uniform. A wide value continuum has developed within our society. The result is conflict. Recently we have seen a phrase introduced into pop culture which names this value conflict—the generation gap. Spindler has diagrammed the value continuum and applied it to the public schools. His research indicates that younger teachers bring with them more emergent values than any other group affiliated with the school, except for the children of emergent parents. To increasing degrees older teachers, school administrators, most of the students, the general public and parents, and the very traditional school boards all hold more traditional values than the first-year teacher. Having come straight from the university, that veritable hot-bed of emergent values, the beginning teacher frequently brings to the school a new gospel which he hopes to preach to the unenlightened. This may, indeed, be what some find most attractive about the teacher's role. But though he comes trailing glory from the university, the older members of the school have difficulty accept-

10. George Spindler, *Education and Culture* (New York: Holt, Rinehart, and Winston, 1963), pp. 132–42.

ing an untested, unseasoned rookie as an emissary of light. This is particularly true when dealing with questions of values. Instead of shedding light among older colleagues and administrators, the value discussions between the beginning teacher and his older colleagues frequently just cause heat. The beginning teacher may be especially prone to value conflicts because of the intensity of his views and because of inexperience in handling value questions with older adults. Perhaps the only real practice he has had is arguing about politics with his parents, an experience from which few come away wiser.

In recent years the normal strains between young adults and older adults, between new teachers and veteran teachers, have been intensified. Perhaps more than at any time since the thirties, the American college student has involved himself in questions of values. He is often vocal in his dissatisfaction with the moral norms of the adult community. Frequently, instead of looking upon mature teachers and administrators as worthy of respect, he looks upon them as causes of the problems.

John Canfield is a case in point. He appears especially concerned with affecting the values surrounding the school community. His efforts to raise value questions and, indeed, to change the values of his students and his colleagues continually led him into conflict with older teachers. Incidentally, John was predestined for conflict, since he chose to wear a beard, which is perceived as the very badge of the emergent value trailblazers.

English and social studies teachers more than others become immersed in value conflicts. Certainly this was the case with Gary Cornog and Linda Corman. Gary worked to have his students transcend their materialistic views of success and the "good life." This effort kept him continually at loggerheads with students. His genteel feud with his student Jack was nothing more than a public clash of value systems.

Linda Corman found herself in the kind of schools where she represented values which were much more traditional than the more emergent values of her students. She was annoyed by their requests to be allowed to smoke in the dark while listening to records. She found distasteful the casual attitude toward sexuality of one of her students. She was put off by the student who tried to date her, knowing full well she was married. Although the permissive school setting in which she spent the last half of her year is hardly typical of the public schools, Linda's conflict is representative of a type which is not uncommon.

Another major source of conflict for the beginning teacher is the disparity between what should be and what is. This is an interior conflict and one which can cost the novice much frustration and disappointment. As mentioned earlier, teacher preparation tends to deal with what ought to be going on in the schools rather than what is actually happening. As a result, the beginning teacher comes to his initial teaching experience well primed about what should ideally go on in the school. He is in touch with the most current thinking concerning the teaching of his subject. He has been exposed to the latest and best texts in his field. He knows the principles of adolescent psychology and the principles of instruction. However, when what he knows "should be" bumps against his actual experience in the schools—inadequate curricula, out-of-date texts, real adolescents, and his own stumbling instruction—tension develops. This tension does not disappear until the teacher either achieves his ideals or lowers his standards. Most are forced to lower standards.

Uncertainty is part of being a first-year teacher. Because he hasn't quite mastered teaching before being given full responsibility for a class, the beginner is naturally uncertain in his performance. Since he lacks the assurance which comes with experience, the beginning teacher must live by the expectations of others. The people around the beginning teacher—administrators, experienced teachers, and students—all have rather definite ideas about what is good teaching. Through a variety of channels, these people get their message to him. Unless by some rare quirk or probability the messages are similar, the first-year teacher will become involved in conflict, because different people with different expectations send different messages. An administrator may perceive him one way and suggest that more attention be given to the enforcement of rules and regulations. Some veteran teachers may be seeking docility and respect from their young colleague. Other experienced teachers may be looking for allies against a department chairman or administrator and may therefore send him very different messages than his supervisors. Students may be sending him a veritable cacophony of messages. Some students, by their enthusiasm and attention and by hundreds of different cues, may be telling the teacher that he is fulfilling their highest expectations. Others, by withdrawal and signs of boredom, may frustrate the teacher's best efforts. And others, by small signs of hostility and disrespect, may be extremely discouraging. If all of these sources of information or feedback relayed the same expectations to the teacher, undoubtedly the messages would not be so confusing and cause such conflict for him.

The conflicts of the first year are a major factor in the new teacher's initiation. They are a great part of that much revered teacher experience. Unfortunately, experiences of conflict in the first year are not uniformly used to help the beginner grow and develop. He learns how to survive and avoid the conflicts, but he does not know how to use them to generate light and change. The bruises and bumps knock off his rough edges so that next year it is easier for him to mesh with the system.

At the end of the first year, few beginners are the teachers they had hoped to become. Linda Corman is not discouraged by her "fifty percent." The first-year teacher's chagrin over his mistakes and disappointments is offset by knowing *he has made it*. He knows he has gone through the fire and survived. He knows his mistakes and has a fairly good idea of how to avoid them next September. He knows he has learned an immense amount about himself.

Besides learning that they are teachers, beginners learn some lesser but still significant things about themselves. They have the very rewarding experience of finding out that they are good at doing things about which they were never aware. Some learn that they are excellent at explaining difficult ideas to students. Others surprise themselves by the discovery that they have a sense of humor to which students are very responsive. Some discover that they are the object of respect and often admiration. Others are pleasantly surprised by their power. "Students actually obey me!" This can be a heady experience for someone who has just spent sixteen or seventeen years as a powerless student. Others find a hidden bit of ham in themselves and get an unholy pleasure out of performing before students. And many fortunate first-year teachers come to the strong realization that teaching is for them. They know that they have made mistakes during their initiation period, but they are confident about next year. Further, they see in teaching a worthwhile life-work which will bring them continuing satisfactions.

Implications for Change

Criticism of "what is" carries with it the silent obligation of stating "what should be." While it is more comfortable to deal with the former, a word about the latter is in order. Obviously, universities and other teacher education institutions need to do a more adequate job of training beginning teachers for the realities of secondary schools. Two things would be helpful here. First, more honesty about what schools are like and the kinds of problems which confront teachers is required. If future teachers had a clearer and better idea of what was really ahead of them, this in itself would be a major step forward. Second, the training institutions should put much more stress on performance training. Right now teacher educators prepare people for the very active role of teacher by treating them as passive agents. The bulk of professional education is made up of sitting in lecture halls, taking notes, and writing paper-and-pencil exams. While this may be an efficient way to learn economic theory, the structure of a sonnet, and the concept of the light-year, it is not a very effective way to prepare someone to teach. Preparing a person for the role of teacher is much different from preparing someone to be a research historian. To learn the dynamic role of teacher, the prospective teacher should have many opportunities to study and practice the skills and strategies of teaching, and he should have real encounters with high school students. If progress is to be made here, universities and schools will have to develop new relationships. Right now the universities act as distant producers of teachers, and public schools act as uncritical consumers. This situation is not unlike the Russians' economic practices during the Stalinist era, when huge, remote factories produced standardized suits with little concern for local desires or consumer needs. We need to forge a new partnership in which teacher training institutions and public schools are in close contact, with each contributing its strengths to the training of teachers.

One thing the schools can do is help overcome the beginning teacher's sense of isolation. The first-year teacher is not only in need of help in coping with his classes, but he also needs support as an individual. At the time in his life when he is going through difficult trials, he is a stranger to the vast numbers of people around him. He needs to be part of a community. This could be accomplished quite easily if beginning teachers were part of special in-service experiences. The beginners could not only teach and learn from one another, but they could also support one another. Such special programs would provide opportunities for veteran teachers and beginners to come together and discuss the many problems that surround educating the young. Instead of viewing one another from a distance and with suspicion, both groups could learn from each other.

We should also abandon the unstated assumption that we can make "instant teachers." Exposing college students to some abstractions about education, giving them a brief experience as student teachers, and certifying them as professionals equipped to meet the demands of the classroom would be ludicrous if the results were not so unfortunate. A more gradual, systematic approach to entrance into the profession should be developed to replace our present "trial by fire" method. College students should go through something along the lines of a two- or three-year residency. During this residence, the teacher in training could be involved in several work assignments in the school, such as tutoring individual students, being a resource person in the library, monitoring study halls, working as a teacher aid or with a team of teachers, instructing small groups of students, and occasionally making presentations to an entire class. The intention, however, would be to give the future teacher a chance both to gain an understanding of the school and to acquire real mastery over some of the component activities of teaching.

The suggestions above are hardly radical. Nor are they new. Many schools have incorporated some of the suggestions into their induction programs for new teachers. The National Association of Secondary School Principals has recently completed a three-year study on induction of beginning teachers under the direction of Douglas W. Hunt.[11] Following the recommendations of James Conant, the NASSP study tested a teacher induction system which was tried out in a number of high schools throughout the nation. The recommendations that grew out of this study are as follows: (1) limited teaching responsibility for the new teacher; (2) aid in gathering instructional materials; (3) advice

11. Douglas W. Hunt, "Opportunity and Responsibility," in *The National Association of Secondary School Principals Bulletin: The Beginning Teacher,* October 1968, pp. 130–35.

of experienced teachers whose own teaching loads are reduced so that they can work with the new teacher in his own classroom; (4) shifting to more experienced teachers those students who create problems beyond the ability of the novice to handle effectively; (5) specialized instruction concerning the character of the community, the neighborhood, and the students he is likely to encounter.

It is quite possible, though, that the bedrock problem with teacher preparation is that people are being trained for an impossible job. It may well be that the learning needs of children can no longer be met effectively in the typical classroom setting. The role of teacher as dispenser of information in the classroom may be inappropriate for children of the electronic age. It is quite possible that growing up with constant saturation and stimulation from television and other electronic media has shaped styles of learning in the young which are out of joint with the instructional modes of the blackboard, the textbook, and the classroom teacher. Maybe all the stress and trauma of the beginner's adjustment to the role of teacher result from the growing lack of fit between our current way of organizing school and what children actually need. Perhaps, then, the real problem of the first-year of teaching is learning how to adapt to an outmoded, archaic way of teaching. Maybe we are teaching teachers to crack a buggy whip in the age of space travel.

Any change in the training of beginning teachers is inextricably bound up with the education of children. And just as awareness of strains encountered by these six beginning teachers should lead us to reexamine the entrance system for teaching, it should also cause us to raise some questions about the secondary schools themselves. Why is there so much hostility in the schools? Why is there so much concern over discipline and order? Why is there such distance between students and teachers? Why are so many students so bored? The search for answers to these questions will undoubtedly raise even more basic questions. Why have we designed the high school experience as we have? Is it necessary to conceive of teaching as being something that happens when an adult faces north and thirty children face south? Why is the school day divided into fifty-minute slices of time? While these units may be occasionally convenient, must the school be frozen by them? And then there are the most fundamental questions,

questions which never get asked—except by students: Why do we continue to teach what we teach? Why history, English, mathematics, foreign language, industrial arts, chemistry, and so on? Is it because we have nothing else to teach? Is it because the colleges insist on it? Because the students want to learn these subjects? Because the young need these subjects to become fully human? Because our present system is designed to legitimatize the hobbies of teachers? Is it not possible that if our present curriculum disappeared one night and we started de novo we might have a very different curriculum? Perhaps we might find both the children and the society demanding such subjects as the nature of man, visual arts, human communications, methods of knowing, and music and the dance.

The first year of teaching is the beginner's initiation into the profession. Like other initiation rites, whether into the role of infantryman or fraternity man, it is a period of intense learning and also of trial. In the same way that mamma's-boys become soldiers and high school boys become fraternity brothers, young adults become teachers. Beyond these major transformations, initiations exert important but subtle changes. In particular, initiations make defenders and believers. This is true of the first-year teacher, too. Somehow the pain, humiliation, and anguish of the experience (and also the exhilaration and triumph of completion) work on the individual. He has learned a great deal. He is proud of having survived the trial and recognizes values in it which were not apparent during the moments of pain. Having passed the test and become, as Gary Cornog acknowledges, "one of them," the survivor is no longer as critical of the system. Although he may spend himself trying to improve the system, he does not raise the basic questions—like those mentioned above—about the very nature of the educational system. This allegiance to the status quo is particularly unhealthy at this time. Presently there is a growing awareness within the larger community that the schools need fundamental changes if they are to be a vital force in the lives of our children. If the beginning teachers are not the agents of reform, the chances for real change are small.